LIVING AS YOURSELF

Travis Brown

ISBN 979-8-89601-342-6 (paperback)
ISBN 979-8-89601-343-3 (digital)

Hawes & Jenkins Publishing
16427 N Scottsdale Road Suite 410
Scottsdale, AZ 85254
www.hawesjenkins.com

Printed in the United States of America

Chapter 1

The Myth of Perfection

A Kid Who Always Felt Unaccepted

Growing up, I always felt like I was standing on the outside looking in, my nose pressed against an invisible glass that separated me from everyone else's seemingly effortless existence. I watched my classmates blend seamlessly into the social fabric of our school as if they had been handed some secret instruction manual at birth—they knew exactly which clothes would earn approving nods, which words would spark the right kind of laughter, which mannerisms would make them appear confident and desirable. They moved through hallways and classrooms with an ease that felt almost magical to my anxious, observing eyes.

And then there was me, perpetually confused and self-conscious, always feeling like I had somehow missed the crucial memo that explained how to navigate teenage social dynamics. I would study their interactions like an anthropologist trying to decode an alien culture, memorizing their gestures and phrases, hoping to crack the code that would finally grant me entry into their world.

But no matter how carefully I observed or how desperately I tried to mimic their behaviors, I didn't fit into the predetermined molds that others seemed to slip into as naturally as putting on a favorite sweater. I was the wrong shape, the wrong texture, always protruding awkwardly from spaces that were clearly designed for someone else entirely.

I remember sitting in the cafeteria during lunch, my eyes methodically scanning the sprawling room for a seat, each table presenting itself like a potential minefield of social rejection. The familiar weight of my lunch tray seemed to grow heavier with each passing second as I stood there, frozen in the doorway, watching the intricate social ecosystem unfold before me.

It was as if there were invisible but impenetrable lines that divided the various groups—thick unspoken boundaries that everyone else seemed to understand instinctively. The sports kids dominated their territory at one long table near the windows, their letterman jackets and confident postures creating an aura of untouchable popularity. The theater kids had claimed their own corner, animated and dramatic even in their casual conversations, their hands gesturing wildly as they discussed weekend rehearsals and upcoming productions. The "cool" kids held court around their coveted corner table, their effortless laughter ringing out across the room like a soundtrack to their seemingly perfect lives.

And there was me, awkward and unsure, pacing the linoleum floor like a lost puzzle piece that didn't quite fit anywhere, my sneakers squeaking softly with each hesitant step as I desperately searched for some small space where I might belong, even temporarily.

I tried. God, how I tried. I really did. Every morning, I would stand in front of my bedroom mirror, carefully selecting clothes that I hoped would help me blend in seamlessly with the crowd. I studied their mannerisms like a foreign language I desperately needed to master, practiced their casual way of speaking until it felt almost natural rolling off my tongue. I even forced myself to laugh at their jokes—the ones I didn't quite understand, the ones that sometimes made me uncomfortable, the ones that felt hollow echoing in my chest.

But nothing ever felt quite right, no matter how perfectly I thought I had mimicked their behavior. It was like wearing a costume that was perpetually the wrong size, always shifting and never quite settling into place. The harder I tried to mold myself into their image, the more artificial and foreign I felt in my own skin.

I was trying to be someone I wasn't, someone I could never authentically become, and paradoxically, it made me feel even more isolated than before. I was surrounded by people—chattering, laughing, living their lives around me—yet somehow I still felt profoundly, achingly alone. The loneliness wasn't just about being by myself; it was about being invisible while standing right in the middle of everything, about feeling disconnected even when I was desperately trying to connect.

Have you ever felt like that? Like no matter how desperately hard you try to fit in, how meticulously you study the social cues and mimic the behaviors around you, it's somehow never quite enough? Like you're perpetually one step behind everyone else, always hovering just outside the invisible circle that seems to form so naturally around others, and no matter what adjustments you make to your personality or appearance, no matter how many times you rehearse conversations in your head or practice smiling in the mirror, you can't quite seem to blend seamlessly into the crowd?

It's that maddening feeling of being so close yet so impossibly far from belonging—like pressing your face against the glass of a warm, inviting house while standing alone in the cold, watching the life and laughter happening just beyond your reach, knowing you're visible but somehow still unseen.

I spent so many years thinking that something was fundamentally, irreparably wrong with me. The messages I received—some delivered with cutting directness, others whispered through subtle glances and casual exclusions—told me in no uncertain terms that I wasn't enough. I wasn't pretty enough, with my unruly hair that refused to cooperate no matter how much product I slathered on it, or my skin that seemed to betray me at the worst possible moments. I wasn't confident enough, stumbling over my words when called upon in class or shrinking into myself whenever I walked into a crowded room. I wasn't smart enough, despite my decent grades, because intelligence seemed to be measured not just by what you knew, but by how effortlessly you could display that knowledge, how naturally you could command attention and respect.

I didn't have the "right" friends—the ones who seemed to glide through social situations with an ease I could only dream of, who knew exactly what to wear and when to laugh and how to make everything look so beautifully, enviably simple. I didn't have the "right" look, whatever that mysterious standard was supposed to be, the one that everyone else seemed to understand intuitively while I floundered in confusion. I felt like I was constantly falling short of some invisible benchmark, like I was playing an increasingly complex game where everyone else had been handed the rulebook while I was left to fumble my way through, making mistake after embarrassing mistake.

The fear of being judged, of being seen as different in all the wrong ways, kept me trapped in this suffocating cycle of self-doubt that seemed to tighten its grip with each passing day. Every sideways glance felt like confirmation of my inadequacy, every moment of silence in conversation felt like evidence of my social failure, every mirror became a harsh judge reflecting back all the ways I didn't measure up to whatever impossible standard I was trying so desperately to reach.

But here's the thing I've come to understand after years of wrestling with these destructive thoughts—every single one of those crushing beliefs was nothing more than an elaborate, convincing lie that my mind had constructed to keep me small and afraid.

I wasn't broken, despite what the relentless voice in my head kept insisting with such cruel persistence. I wasn't fundamentally flawed in some irreparable way that set me apart from the rest of humanity. I wasn't defective or damaged goods that somehow slipped through quality control. I just wasn't like everyone else, and slowly, painfully, beautifully, I began to realize that this difference wasn't a curse to bear—it was perfectly, wonderfully okay.

The real problem, the source of all this anguish and self-torment, wasn't me at all. The problem was this suffocating, impossible myth of perfection that had somehow wrapped itself around my consciousness like a parasitic vine, choking out any possibility of self-acceptance or genuine peace.

Breaking the Myth of Perfection

When I reflect on those turbulent formative years, I realize with startling clarity just how much relentless pressure we're all under to fit into a certain predetermined mold that society has carefully crafted for us. Society—through the endless scroll of social media feeds, the glossy manipulation of advertising campaigns, and even the casual yet cutting remarks from our peers—systematically creates and reinforces this suffocating idea of exactly what we should look like, how we should act, and who we should fundamentally be at our core.

We're constantly fed these carefully curated, airbrushed images of absolute perfection: flawless, poreless skin that seems to glow from within, the perfect body with impossible proportions that defies basic human anatomy, the perfect life filled with designer clothes, exotic vacations, and perpetual happiness without a single moment of genuine struggle or authentic vulnerability.

It's devastatingly easy to believe, when bombarded with these manufactured ideals day after day, that if we don't somehow manage to meet those impossibly high, constantly shifting standards, then something must be fundamentally, irreparably wrong with us. We internalize these toxic messages so deeply that they become the cruel inner voice that whispers lies about our worth, our value, and our right to take up space in this world.

But the devastating truth that took me years to fully comprehend and accept is that perfection—this elusive, shimmering mirage we're all desperately chasing—simply doesn't exist anywhere in the realm of human experience. It's nothing more than a carefully constructed myth, a brilliantly marketed illusion that has been sold to us through generations of conditioning and manipulation. Perfection is an artificial construct, a moving target that we, as flawed and beautifully imperfect human beings, can never truly attain no matter how hard we strive, how much we sacrifice, or how relentlessly we push ourselves toward these impossible ideals.

And yet despite the logical understanding that perfection is unattainable, so many of us continue to chase this phantom with desperate intensity, pouring our energy, our self-worth, and our precious time into this futile pursuit. We convince ourselves with unwavering determination that once we finally reach that magical state of perfection—once we achieve that flawless appearance, that ideal weight, that perfect relationship, that dream career—we'll finally feel complete, worthy, and whole. We tell ourselves that all our pain, all our self-doubt, all our feelings of inadequacy will simply vanish the moment we cross that finish line.

But here's the cruel irony that cuts to the very heart of this deception: It's precisely that relentless, all-consuming pursuit of an impossible standard that leaves us feeling more fragmented, more lost, and more disconnected from our authentic selves than ever before.

As a young child navigating the complex social dynamics of school and playground hierarchies, I didn't possess the wisdom or emotional maturity to understand this fundamental truth about human nature and self-acceptance. My innocent mind was consumed with a singular desperate belief that if I could somehow transform myself into a carbon copy of everyone else around me—if I could successfully mold myself into their exact image, adopt their mannerisms, mirror their interests, and seamlessly blend into their established groups—then I would finally, inevitably be welcomed with open arms into that coveted circle of acceptance and belonging that seemed so effortlessly available to others.

But despite my relentless efforts to contort myself into those rigid, predetermined cookie-cutter shapes that society seemed to demand, despite the exhausting mental gymnastics I performed daily to suppress my natural instincts and authentic responses, I consistently found myself falling woefully short of those impossible standards. Every attempt to fit in felt forced and unnatural, like trying to squeeze my entire being into a container that was fundamentally the wrong size and shape for who I truly was.

It wasn't until years later, as I matured and gained the perspective that only comes with experience and self-reflection, that a profound realization began to dawn on me with startling clarity: My uniqueness, those very qualities that made me different from everyone else, wasn't something to desperately hide away in shame or feel deeply embarrassed about. Instead, it was something precious and valuable to celebrate, cherish, and embrace with pride and confidence.

The truth I discovered—through my own painful struggles, countless mistakes, and years of trying to force myself into molds that were never meant for me—is that you don't need to fit in with the crowd or conform to everyone else's expectations. You don't need to be perfect, flawless, or have all the answers figured out before you can feel worthy of love and acceptance.

What you truly need to do, what will ultimately set you free and bring you genuine peace, is to fully embrace who you are at your core. Your quirks, those little idiosyncrasies that make you laugh at inappropriate moments or see the world from an entirely different angle—they're not flaws to be corrected. Your oddities, the way you think differently or approach problems with unconventional solutions—they're not mistakes to be ashamed of. Your differences, all those characteristics that set you apart from the mainstream and make you stand out in a crowd—they are precisely what make you who you are, in all your authentic, unfiltered glory.

And that authentic version of yourself? That's exactly what this world desperately needs, craves, and is waiting for you to share.

Exercise: Reframing a "Flaw"

Now let's take a moment to pause and reflect deeply on something you've always perceived as a fundamental flaw or something you genuinely don't like about yourself. This might be something physical—perhaps the way you look in photographs, the shape of your nose, or how your hair never seems to cooperate no matter what products you try. It could be a personality trait you desperately wish you didn't possess—maybe you're someone who speaks too quickly when nervous, or you have a tendency to overthink every conversation hours after it's ended.

Perhaps it's something about your character that consistently makes you feel "different" from everyone around you—the way you process emotions more intensely than others, how you need more time alone to recharge, or how you approach problems in ways that seem to confuse your peers. Whatever it is that comes to mind first, that nagging voice that whispers you're somehow not quite right, take a moment to acknowledge it without judgment.

Write it down honestly, without filtering or softening the edges. Allow yourself to name this thing you've been carrying, this aspect of yourself that you've been trying to hide, minimize, or change for far too long.

Now let's fundamentally challenge that deeply ingrained thought pattern. In the quiet space below, I want you to take a different lens—one of curiosity rather than criticism—and write down three specific ways this perceived "flaw" actually contributes something meaningful and positive to your life, or explore how it has gradually shaped you in ways that foster genuine growth and resilience.

Consider this reframing exercise with genuine openness. For example, perhaps you've always believed you're far too introverted compared to your more outgoing friends and colleagues, constantly wishing you could be the life of the party. But when you shift your perspective, you might recognize that this very quality grants you an extraordinary depth of introspection, allowing you to process experiences more thoroughly and develop a rare ability to truly listen to others—skills that make you someone people naturally gravitate toward when they need genuine understanding.

Maybe you've spent years convinced that you're simply too sensitive for this harsh world, that your emotional responses are excessive compared to those around you. Yet this heightened sensitivity might be precisely what enables you to offer unparalleled compassion to friends in crisis, to notice subtle changes in others' moods that everyone else misses, and to create deeper, more authentic connections that many people spend their entire lives searching for.

We all carry within us a catalogue of things we desperately wish were different about ourselves—those persistent internal criticisms that whisper we're somehow lacking or inadequate. Perhaps it's the way we stumble over words in social situations or how we retreat into ourselves when others seem to effortlessly command attention. Maybe it's our tendency to overthink every decision or the way our emotions feel too big, too raw, too present in a world that seems to prize composure above all else.

But something remarkable happens when we deliberately shift our perspective and reframe those relentless thoughts of inadequacy. We begin to see, often with startling clarity, that our so-called flaws aren't actually flaws at all. They're not mistakes in our design or evidence of our unworthiness. Instead, they're integral threads woven into the fabric of who we are—distinctive qualities that set us apart from the homogeneous crowd and contribute to our individual brilliance.

These perceived imperfections, when viewed through a lens of acceptance rather than judgment, reveal themselves to be the very elements that make us irreplaceably unique. They're what give us our particular flavor, our distinctive voice in the grand chorus of humanity. Ultimately, they're precisely what make us not just special, but essential—bringing something to the world that no one else can offer in quite the same way.

Final Thought: You Are Not Broken

I want you to know this, and I want you to feel it deep in your bones: There is absolutely nothing wrong with you. You're not broken, despite what the whispers of self-doubt might suggest in your quieter moments. You're not incomplete, even when you catch yourself measuring your worth against impossible standards. You're not damaged goods waiting to be fixed or a rough draft in need of endless revision.

You are exactly, precisely, unequivocally as you were meant to be. Every quirk, every sensitivity, every moment of uncertainty—they're all part of your authentic design. The myth of perfection, with its glossy promises and relentless demands, may try to convince you otherwise. It may whisper that you need to sand down your edges, dim your intensity, or conform to some predetermined mold of acceptability.

But here's the truth that matters most: It's entirely up to you to rewrite your story. You hold the pen. You get to choose whether to believe the narrative of inadequacy or to author a new chapter—one that celebrates your wholeness, honors your journey, and recognizes that you've been complete all along.

You don't need to transform yourself into someone else's vision of acceptability to earn your place in this world. You don't need to shed the very qualities that make you uniquely you, dimming your light to make others more comfortable. You don't need to contort yourself into shapes that feel foreign and uncomfortable, twisting your essence to fit into spaces that were never meant for you anyway.

The truth is beautifully simple: You are enough, exactly as you are in this very moment. Not the version of yourself you think you should become, not the polished persona you present when you're trying too hard, but the real, unfiltered, sometimes messy, always authentic you. Your worth isn't contingent on meeting someone else's criteria or checking boxes on an invisible list of requirements.

And here's where something truly extraordinary begins to unfold—when you finally stop running from yourself and instead turn toward who you really are with open arms, when you begin to accept every facet of your being with genuine compassion, when you choose to embrace your authentic self with all its perceived flaws and undeniable brilliance, that's precisely when the real magic happens. That's when life stops feeling like an exhausting performance and starts feeling like coming home.

In the next chapter, we'll delve deeper into the transformative journey of embracing your unique qualities—those distinctive traits, quirks, and characteristics that make you who you are. We'll explore how to shift your perspective and begin seeing these aspects of yourself not as imperfections to be hidden or corrected, not as flaws that diminish your worth or make you somehow less deserving of love and acceptance but as genuine strengths that contribute to the beautiful, complex, wonderfully individual person you are. These qualities aren't mistakes or accidents—they're the very threads that weave together the tapestry of your authentic self.

We'll discover how your sensitivity, which you might have been told is too much, is actually a superpower that allows you to connect deeply with others and experience life with profound richness. We'll uncover how your unconventional way of thinking, the very thing that might have made you feel like an outsider, is precisely what enables you to offer fresh perspectives and innovative solutions. We'll learn to celebrate the qualities that make you different, recognizing them as gifts rather than burdens.

But for now, in this quiet moment before we continue this journey together, I want you to remember this fundamental truth and let it settle deep into your bones: You belong. Just as you are, in all your glorious imperfection and radiant authenticity. You belong in this world, in your relationships, in the spaces you occupy. Your presence matters, your voice deserves to be heard, and your unique way of being adds something irreplaceable to the human experience.

Chapter 2

Embracing Your Unique Qualities

Celebrating What Makes You Different

In the previous chapter, we delved deep into how the relentless pressure to conform and fit into predetermined molds can leave us feeling fundamentally unworthy and inadequate. The uncomfortable truth is we often find ourselves trapped in the suffocating idea that there exists a singular "right" way to be—a narrow definition carefully constructed from rigid societal standards, deeply ingrained cultural norms, or even the subtle yet persistent expectations of our friends and family members. We internalize these external pressures until they become our own harsh inner critics, constantly measuring ourselves against impossible standards.

But what if I told you that the secret to genuine happiness and fulfillment doesn't lie in desperately trying to squeeze yourself into someone else's definition of acceptable? What if the very key to unlocking your true potential lies in courageously embracing who you truly are, complete with all your beautiful quirks, distinctive perspectives, and wonderful uniqueness that makes you irreplaceably you?

It's remarkably easy to feel like something is fundamentally wrong when we're not "like everyone else," but I want you to know something with absolute certainty: Your differences are your strengths. This isn't just empty reassurance or feel-good platitudes—it's a truth I've learned through years of struggling with my own sense of not belonging.

I used to genuinely believe there was something deeply wrong with me for being the way I am. I wasn't the loudest person in any room or the most naturally outgoing individual who could effortlessly command attention at social gatherings. I didn't have what society deemed a perfect body, with all the right curves in all the right places, and I certainly wasn't the most fashionable person in any room, always seeming to miss the mark when it came to current trends and styles that everyone else seemed to instinctively understand.

Instead, I was quiet by nature, deeply introspective in a world that seemed to value quick answers and instant reactions, and incredibly sensitive to the emotions and energies around me—traits that didn't always align with what I saw portrayed as ideal in movies, magazines, or even in the people I admired from afar. I felt like I was constantly swimming upstream against a current of expectations that seemed designed for someone completely different from who I was.

But as I gradually matured and gained more life experience, I began to have a profound realization that would fundamentally shift my entire perspective on myself: My natural introversion, which I had always viewed as a social handicap, actually granted me the extraordinary ability to sit back and truly observe the intricate dynamics of human behavior. While others were busy filling every silence with chatter or rushing to be the center of attention, I was quietly watching, listening, and absorbing the subtle nuances of how people interacted with one another.

My heightened sensitivity to emotions and energy, which had once felt like an overwhelming burden that left me drained after social interactions, gradually revealed itself to be an incredible gift that allowed me to connect with others on a remarkably deep and meaningful level. I could sense when someone was struggling beneath their cheerful facade, pick up on the unspoken tensions in a room, and offer comfort to those who needed it most—often before they even realized they needed it themselves.

Those very traits that I had spent years viewing as fundamental flaws in my character, as evidence that I was somehow broken or defective compared to everyone else, slowly transformed in my understanding to become my greatest strengths and most valuable assets.

You may find yourself thinking, "But I'm not like everyone else either. What makes me unique doesn't seem particularly special or remarkable." I understand that feeling completely, having wrestled with those same doubts for years. Trust me when I say with absolute certainty, it is special—profoundly so. You possess qualities, perspectives, and ways of being that no one else in this world has ever had or ever will have. These aren't just minor differences or surface-level variations; they are the fundamental essence of what makes you irreplaceably you.

The combination of your experiences, your thought patterns, your emotional responses, and your unique way of processing the world around you creates something entirely original. Even if you share certain traits with others, the specific way these characteristics blend together in you is completely unprecedented. Your particular brand of humor, the way you solve problems, how you show compassion, or the perspective you bring to conversations—these are gifts that only you can offer to the world.

The Power of Embracing Your Quirks

Embracing your unique qualities starts with the fundamental step of recognizing and acknowledging them. This process requires honest self-reflection and a willingness to look beyond society's narrow definitions of what's considered "normal" or "valuable." What are the specific things that make you distinctly different from others around you?

Is it the particular way your mind processes information and thinks about the world—perhaps you approach problems from unexpected angles or you notice patterns that others miss entirely? Maybe it's the distinctive way you express yourself, whether through your choice of words, your creative outlets, or even the subtle mannerisms that are uniquely yours. Could it be the passionate intensity with which you view your interests, diving deeper into subjects that fascinate you while others might only scratch the surface?

These differences aren't flaws to be corrected or minimized—they're the raw materials from which your greatest contributions to the world will emerge. The very things that once made you feel like an outsider are often the same qualities that will eventually set you apart as someone truly remarkable.

We live in a world that often tries to categorize people into neat, predictable boxes—labeling us according to standardized metrics and conventional expectations. Society has a tendency to create templates for how we should look, think, behave, and even feel, as if there were some universal blueprint for human existence that we're all supposed to follow.

But the truth is there is no one-size-fits-all approach to who we are or who we're meant to become. Your quirks—whether they manifest as physical characteristics that don't conform to traditional beauty standards, emotional responses that seem more intense or different from those around you, or intellectual patterns that lead you down unexpected pathways of thought—are precisely what make you stand out in the world in meaningful and irreplaceable ways.

These distinctive traits of yours add vibrant splashes of color to what would otherwise be a monochrome canvas of conformity. They create texture and depth in the human experience, contributing layers of complexity and richness that make life infinitely more interesting and beautiful than it would be if we all followed the same prescribed patterns of existence.

For example, one of my most pronounced quirks is that I think deeply and analytically about almost everything that crosses my path. It's a trait that used to make me feel profoundly distant and disconnected from others, as if I were operating on a completely different wavelength from the rest of the world. People around me would be quick to jump to conclusions or make snap decisions on the spot, trusting their gut instincts and moving forward with confidence, while I would be the one sitting quietly in the corner, methodically overthinking every possible angle, considering all the potential consequences, and analyzing the situation from multiple perspectives before even beginning to form an opinion.

For a long time, this tendency made me feel strange, awkward, and utterly out of place in social situations. I would watch others navigate conversations and decisions with what seemed like effortless ease while I remained trapped in my own head, wrestling with complexities that others didn't seem to notice or care about. I began to believe that this reflective nature was a burden, a flaw that prevented me from connecting with people in the spontaneous, carefree way that seemed to come so naturally to everyone else.

But now I realize that this deep, contemplative approach to life is actually my superpower—it gives me invaluable perspective, hard-earned wisdom, and a uniquely thorough way of solving problems that others might miss entirely. What I once saw as a limitation has become one of my greatest strengths.

Your quirks, those distinctive traits that set you apart from the crowd, are truly your personal superpowers in disguise. They represent the unique combination of characteristics, perspectives, and approaches that only you possess—the very things that make you an irreplaceable and valuable contribution to the fabric of humanity. Rather than viewing these differences as obstacles to overcome or flaws to hide, they should be celebrated as the extraordinary gifts they truly are.

It's not about molding yourself to fit into someone else's predetermined box or conforming to what society tells you is normal or acceptable. Instead, it's about having the courage to stand out boldly in your own beautifully authentic way, owning every aspect of what makes you distinctly you, and recognizing that the world needs exactly what you have to offer—not a watered-down version of yourself but the full, unfiltered, magnificent truth of who you are.

A Celebration of Differences

Imagine for a moment if the world was populated entirely by people who were all exactly the same—carbon copies of one another with identical thoughts, perspectives, dreams, and ways of approaching life's countless challenges. There would be no diversity of thought to spark meaningful debates, no different perspectives to illuminate hidden truths, no clash of ideas to generate breakthrough innovations, and no unique viewpoints to solve complex problems in unexpected ways. Every conversation would echo the same predictable patterns, every solution would follow the same well-worn paths, and every creative endeavor would produce the same uninspired results.

Life would be remarkably dull, wouldn't it? The very fabric of human experience would lose its rich texture, its surprising twists and turns, its beautiful complexity that comes from the wonderful collision of different minds, hearts, and souls working together to create something far greater than the sum of its parts.

What makes our world truly vibrant and alive is the incredible variety of people, experiences, and viewpoints that weave together to create the rich tapestry of human existence. Your uniqueness—every single aspect of who you are—contributes an irreplaceable thread to that magnificent tapestry. The way you think and process information, the way you express love and compassion to those around you, the way you approach challenges and problem-solve with your own distinct perspective—all these qualities and countless others form the essence of your special place in this world.

Each person brings something different to the table: a unique lens through which they view life's complexities, a distinctive voice that adds to the grand conversation of humanity, and a particular set of gifts that no one else possesses in quite the same combination. Your individual way of moving through the world, of connecting with others, of finding meaning and purpose—these aren't just random characteristics, but essential elements that help create the beautiful diversity that makes life so wonderfully unpredictable and enriching.

It's remarkably easy to fall into the trap of believing that we need to fundamentally alter who we are at our core to gain acceptance from others, to fit into social circles, or to meet the expectations that society places upon us. This pressure can feel overwhelming at times, leading us to suppress our natural instincts, hide our authentic thoughts and feelings, or adopt personas that feel foreign and uncomfortable. We might find ourselves constantly second-guessing our reactions, our preferences, our ways of being in the world, all in pursuit of some elusive ideal of what we think others want us to be.

But there's profound wisdom and liberation in learning to embrace our differences—those very qualities that set us apart from the crowd. When we stop fighting against our natural tendencies and instead lean into what makes us distinctive, something beautiful happens: We discover a deeper, more genuine sense of belonging that doesn't require us to sacrifice who we are. This isn't about fitting into a predetermined mold, but rather about finding our tribe, our people, our place in the world where our authentic self is not just tolerated but celebrated.

The truth that bears repeating, again and again, is that you don't have to transform yourself into someone else's image of perfection to be worthy of love, respect, and acceptance. You don't need to mirror anyone else's personality, adopt their mannerisms, or suppress your own voice to have value in this world. Your worthiness isn't contingent upon meeting external standards or conforming to others' expectations. You're already enough, exactly as you are, with all your quirks, complexities, and beautiful imperfections intact.

Exercise: Create Your "Uniqueness List"

Now take a moment to pause and truly celebrate the magnificent tapestry of your individuality. Find a quiet space where you can reflect without distraction and write down a comprehensive list of traits, qualities, or behaviors that make you unmistakably, authentically you. These can be absolutely anything that comes to mind—from the distinctive way you approach challenges and problem-solve to a physical feature that you've always thought of as different or unusual, to a particular quirk or habit that consistently sets you apart from others around you.

Don't hold back or edit yourself during this process. Include the way you laugh when something genuinely amuses you, how you organize your thoughts when making decisions, the unique perspective you bring to conversations, or even the specific way you move through the world. Think about your spontaneous reactions, your thoughtful responses, the subjects that captivate your attention, and the methods you use to express yourself creatively or emotionally.

Here are a few examples to get you started:

After you've made your list, take a moment to truly examine it with fresh eyes and see how each quality is a profound reflection of who you authentically are at your core. How does each of these distinctive traits help you connect with the world around you in your own beautifully special way? Consider how your particular combination of characteristics creates a unique lens through which you experience life, relationships, and the countless small moments that make up your daily existence. Think about how these qualities might serve as bridges to others who share similar perspectives, or how they might offer something entirely different and valuable to those whose experiences contrast with your own.

Reframing Your "Flaws" as Strengths

When you look at the traits that make you unique, take a moment to carefully examine and thoughtfully reframe any perceived "flaws" you may have identified about yourself. What characteristics do you genuinely believe represent weaknesses or shortcomings in your personality? What aspects of your nature do you find yourself apologizing for or trying to hide from others? Now let's pose this transformative question: How could each of these supposed flaws actually be a remarkable strength cleverly disguised, waiting to be recognized and appreciated for the valuable qualities they truly represent?

For example:

Instead of dwelling on how you don't measure up to some arbitrary "ideal" that society has constructed, shift your attention to the remarkable ways these distinctive qualities provide you with a completely unique lens through which to view and understand the world. Your particular combination of traits—whether it's your sensitivity, your introversion, your unconventional thinking patterns, or your deep capacity for empathy—creates a perspective that is entirely your own, one that allows you to see nuances and possibilities that others might completely overlook.

These qualities don't just make you different; they make you essential. They contribute to the world in their own profound and powerful way, offering insights, solutions, and understanding that can only come from someone who experiences life exactly as you do. Your unique perspective becomes a gift not just to yourself but to everyone whose life you touch through your authentic way of being.

Final Thought: The Beauty of Being Different

At the end of the day, beneath all our ambitions and desires, we all share that fundamental human longing to belong somewhere, to find our tribe, to feel genuinely accepted and valued. But here's the beautiful paradox that so many of us miss: The most authentic and lasting way to find true belonging isn't by contorting yourself to fit into spaces that were never meant for you, but rather by courageously embracing and celebrating your unique qualities with unwavering confidence.

When you finally stop apologizing for who you are and instead begin to embrace your distinctive traits—your quirks, your perspectives, your particular way of moving through the world—something almost magical begins to unfold. You start to naturally attract the right people and opportunities into your life, as if the universe itself is responding to your newfound authenticity. These aren't the people who tolerate your differences or ask you to dim your light; these are the people who see your uniqueness and think, "Yes, this is exactly what we've been missing."

You stop exhausting yourself with the endless performance of pretending to be someone you're not, constantly monitoring and adjusting your behavior to match what you think others expect. Instead, you begin living in genuine alignment with who you truly are at your core, and that alignment creates a sense of ease and flow that touches every aspect of your existence.

Remember, you don't have to squeeze yourself into the suffocating mold of conformity or bend yourself into unnatural shapes to fit in with the crowd. The crowd, when you really think about it, is predictable and mundane anyway—a sea of sameness where genuine connection becomes nearly impossible because everyone is too busy performing their assigned roles.

The real magic, the kind that transforms your entire experience of being alive, happens when you finally make the brave decision to embrace your individuality with fierce conviction. When you stop hiding the parts of yourself that make you different and instead showcase them like precious gems, something extraordinary begins to shift in your world.

In doing so, you'll discover that you naturally magnetize the people and places that don't just tolerate your authentic self but actively celebrate you for exactly who you are—quirks, contradictions, and all the beautiful complexity that makes you irreplaceably you.

In the upcoming chapter, we'll delve deep into the transformative practice of ending the exhausting cycle of constant comparison with others—that relentless measuring of your worth against someone else's highlight reel. We'll explore why breaking free from this comparison trap represents such a fundamental and crucial step on your journey toward genuine, unshakeable self-acceptance.

But for this moment, right here and now, I want you to pause and truly absorb this essential truth: Take immense pride in being uniquely, authentically, and unapologetically you. It's precisely this distinctive combination of traits, experiences, perspectives, and qualities that sets you apart from every other person who has ever walked this earth—and it's exactly what makes you genuinely powerful in ways you're only beginning to understand.

Chapter 3

Letting Go of Comparison

The Trap of Comparison

Have you ever caught yourself mindlessly scrolling through social media late at night, your thumb moving automatically across the screen as you absorb image after image of someone else's seemingly perfect life? There you are, perhaps still in your pajamas with unwashed hair and yesterday's worries weighing on your mind, staring at carefully curated photos of exotic vacations, flawless skin, and beaming smiles that seem to mock your own reality. That familiar knot forms in your stomach as you inevitably begin to feel like your own life doesn't measure up to the polished perfection displayed before you.

Maybe you've found yourself comparing your appearance to the filtered, professionally lit selfies that flood your feed—wondering why your skin doesn't glow like theirs, why your body doesn't look as toned, why you can't seem to achieve that effortless beauty that others seem to possess naturally. Or perhaps you've scrutinized your career against the LinkedIn posts celebrating promotions, new job announcements, and professional achievements, leaving you questioning whether you're falling behind in some invisible race you never signed up for.

Your relationships, too, become subject to this relentless comparison. You see the anniversary posts filled with romantic gestures, the family photos that radiate happiness, the friend groups that seem to have endless fun together, and suddenly your own connections feel inadequate or incomplete. This tendency to measure your life against others is such a natural human impulse, wired into our social DNA from our earliest ancestors who survived by understanding their place within the group. Yet in our modern world, this once-useful instinct has transformed into something incredibly toxic and self-destructive.

We live in a world where comparison has become an inescapable constant, a relentless backdrop to our daily existence where it feels like everyone else has somehow cracked the code to a perfect life—they possess better looks with that effortless radiance we can never quite achieve, they've attained more success in their careers while we struggle to find our footing, they maintain better relationships that seem to flow with an ease we've never experienced, and they appear to be living genuinely happier lives filled with joy and contentment that feels perpetually out of our reach.

We scroll through their carefully curated highlights, those perfectly captured moments that represent the very best of their existence, and we make the fatal assumption that everyone else is living this picture-perfect life around the clock. We absorb these polished snapshots as if they represent the complete truth of someone's reality, forgetting that we're only seeing the moments they've chosen to share with the world.

And then inevitably, the destructive inner dialogue begins: What's fundamentally wrong with me? Why don't I have that same success, that same happiness, that same apparent ease with which they navigate through life? Why does everyone else seem to have figured out something that continues to elude me?

The thing is, comparison is never fair because it operates on fundamentally flawed premises. You're comparing your behind-the-scenes reality—the messy, unfiltered, unedited version of your daily life with all its mundane struggles, private moments of doubt, and ordinary Tuesday afternoons—to someone else's carefully crafted highlight reel, those meticulously selected and polished moments that represent only the very peak experiences of their existence.

And what you see through this distorted lens isn't always the truth, nor is it even close to representing the full spectrum of someone's actual lived experience. Social media platforms, in particular, have fundamentally distorted our collective perception of reality in ways that are both subtle and profoundly damaging. We strategically post the absolute best moments of our lives—the celebrations, the achievements, the picture-perfect vacation shots, the milestone announcements—but we rarely, if ever, post about the struggles that keep us awake at night, the failures that make us question our worth, the bad days when we can barely get out of bed, or the ordinary moments of boredom and dissatisfaction that actually make up the majority of human existence.

This selective sharing creates a false impression that everyone else is perpetually thriving, constantly achieving, and living in a state of unending happiness and success while you feel like you're hopelessly stuck in the mud, unable to move forward or make meaningful progress in your own life.

But the devastating truth is, comparison doesn't just harm your self-esteem or damage your confidence in isolated moments; it systematically keeps you trapped in an endless vicious cycle of insecurity and self-doubt that becomes increasingly difficult to break free from as time goes on. When you constantly measure your worth, your achievements, your progress, and your very existence against the lives and accomplishments of others, you will inevitably always come up short in some way or another.

The mathematics of comparison are inherently flawed and cruel. You'll either feel temporarily superior and smugly satisfied when you believe you're winning the imaginary competition you've created in your mind, or you'll feel crushingly inferior, inadequate, and deeply disappointed when you inevitably don't measure up to someone else's perceived success. Both emotional states are toxic and destructive to your well-being, creating an exhausting emotional rollercoaster that leaves you perpetually unsettled and never truly at peace with yourself or your circumstances.

This relentless cycle of comparison becomes a prison of your own making, where the bars are forged from your own insecurities and the key to freedom lies in learning to appreciate your own unique journey without constantly looking over your shoulder at everyone else's path.

Why You Should Stop Comparing Yourself

Here's something profound to truly contemplate and internalize: Your journey through life is fundamentally and irreversibly not their journey, and it never will be. You are not locked in some fierce, relentless competition with anyone else in this world but yourself—the person you were yesterday, last month, or last year. Your path forward is utterly unique to you, distinctively shaped and molded by your personal experiences, your deeply held values and beliefs, and your individual aspirations and dreams for the future.

No one else walking this earth has encountered the exact same combination of circumstances, challenges, opportunities, setbacks, triumphs, and defining moments that have sculpted who you are today. No one else carries your specific blend of talents, weaknesses, perspectives, and life lessons learned through years of living, struggling, growing, and evolving into the person you've become.

The circumstances that have formed your character—the family dynamics you grew up with, the education you received, the relationships that have influenced you, the failures that taught you resilience, the successes that built your confidence—these are yours alone. They cannot be replicated, copied, or experienced by anyone else in quite the same way, making your journey through life an entirely original story that deserves to be honored rather than constantly measured against someone else's completely different narrative.

Every time you catch yourself comparing your life, your achievements, your appearance, or your circumstances to someone else's carefully curated public image, you unconsciously diminish and devalue your own inherent worth as a human being. In those moments of comparison, you temporarily forget—or perhaps deliberately ignore—the fundamental truth that you possess your own distinctive combination of unique strengths, talents, and capabilities, as well as your own specific set of challenges, obstacles, and areas where growth is still needed.

The stark reality that we must all come to terms with is that every single person walking this earth carries their own private struggles, their own hidden battles, their own moments of doubt and vulnerability—deep, personal things that others simply cannot see from their external vantage point. These internal struggles remain carefully hidden behind polished social media profiles, confident public personas, and the natural human tendency to present our best face to the world while keeping our most difficult moments private and protected from public scrutiny.

No one—absolutely no one—is truly perfect, flawless, or without significant challenges, regardless of how effortlessly successful, perpetually happy, or completely put-together their life might appear when viewed from the outside looking in. The image we see of others is often just a carefully selected highlight reel, a curated collection of their best moments, biggest accomplishments, and most photogenic experiences, rather than a complete, honest, and comprehensive picture of their entire human experience with all its complexities, contradictions, and inevitable imperfections.

The fundamental problem with falling into the destructive cycle of comparison is that it systematically and relentlessly robs you of the genuine joy, contentment, and satisfaction that should naturally flow from your own unique life experience. When you find yourself constantly preoccupied with measuring your achievements, progress, and worth against the perceived successes and accomplishments of others, you inevitably miss out on recognizing and truly appreciating the inherent beauty, meaning, and deep fulfillment that comes with embracing your authentic self and living in alignment with your own values, dreams, and personal definition of what makes life worthwhile.

This constant external focus creates a perpetual state of dissatisfaction, where you become so consumed with watching what everyone else is doing, achieving, or possessing that you lose sight of your own remarkable journey, your own meaningful victories, and your own profound moments of growth and self-discovery.

The Power of Focusing on Your Own Journey

Let's make a deliberate and conscious effort to shift our entire perspective and mindset. Instead of constantly looking outward toward others and their achievements, accomplishments, and seemingly perfect lives, let's turn our attention inward toward ourselves and our own remarkable journey. How can you genuinely celebrate and honor your own progress, no matter how incremental or modest it might appear? How can you begin to truly appreciate and recognize the unique gifts, talents, abilities, and perspectives that you bring to the world—those distinctive qualities that make you irreplaceable and valuable in ways that no one else can replicate?

This inward focus requires intentional practice and patience with yourself. It means taking the time to acknowledge your growth, even when it feels slow or imperceptible. It means recognizing that your contributions matter, whether they're grand gestures that change the world or quiet acts of kindness that touch a single life.

When you finally make the conscious decision to stop comparing yourself to others and their seemingly perfect achievements, you can truly begin to live an authentic and fulfilling life. You can genuinely appreciate where you are in this very moment, who you are becoming as a person, and how remarkably far you've traveled on your unique journey of self-discovery and personal development. Your accomplishments, no matter how small, modest, or insignificant they may appear to the outside world or even to your own critical inner voice, are absolutely worth celebrating and honoring because they are a direct reflection of your personal growth, your resilience in the face of challenges, and your unwavering commitment to becoming the best version of yourself.

This shift in perspective allows you to recognize that every step forward, every lesson learned, and every moment of courage you've demonstrated has contributed to the person you are today. Whether it's finally speaking up in a meeting, completing a project you've been putting off, or simply choosing kindness over criticism in your self-talk, these victories deserve acknowledgment and appreciation.

It's also profoundly important to understand and internalize the fact that success is not a one-size-fits-all concept, despite what society, social media, or well-meaning family members might suggest. Your personal idea and vision of what constitutes true success might look completely different from someone else's definition, and that's not just okay—it's absolutely beautiful and necessary for authentic living.

Perhaps your version of success involves finding deep contentment in a quiet, stable life surrounded by loved ones while someone else's success means climbing the corporate ladder or building a global empire. Maybe your success is measured by the quality of relationships you've cultivated, the peace you've found within yourself, or the positive impact you've made in your local community, rather than by salary figures, prestigious titles, or public recognition.

Your success is defined by you and you alone based on your values, your dreams, your circumstances, and what truly brings meaning and fulfillment to your unique existence. This understanding liberates you from the exhausting pursuit of goals that were never truly yours to begin with.

Exercise: A Week Without Comparison

Here's an exercise that will fundamentally transform your relationship with comparison and help you break free from this destructive mental trap once and for all. It's deceptively simple in concept yet incredibly powerful in its impact and lasting effects: For one full week—seven complete days—make a deliberate, conscious, and sustained effort to avoid comparing yourself to anyone else, whether that's friends, colleagues, strangers on the internet, or even family members.

This exercise requires genuine commitment and mindful awareness throughout each day. You'll need to catch yourself in those automatic moments when your mind starts to drift toward comparison—those split seconds when you see someone's accomplishment, lifestyle, or appearance and immediately begin measuring it against your own situation. The goal is to interrupt that habitual pattern before it takes root and redirects your mental energy toward something more constructive and self-affirming.

By taking this deliberate and conscious step away from comparison, you'll gradually begin to see with startling clarity that your inherent value as a person is not tied to, dependent upon, or diminished by anyone else's life circumstances, achievements, or apparent successes. You can finally stop measuring your worth by the arbitrary and often misleading yardstick of others' lives—those carefully curated social media highlights, professional accomplishments, or material possessions that tell only a fraction of their complete story.

Instead, you can begin the liberating process of creating your own authentic and personally meaningful measure of success, one that honors your unique values, circumstances, and aspirations. This shift allows you to define what fulfillment truly looks like for you, whether that's finding deeper connections with loved ones, pursuing creative passions, making a positive impact in your community, or simply finding greater peace and contentment in your daily life.

Reframing Comparison

Now let's take this transformative journey a step further and explore an even more profound shift in perspective. What if you could fundamentally change your relationship with others' achievements? What if instead of that familiar pang of inadequacy or the bitter taste of envy that so often accompanies witnessing someone else's triumph, you could genuinely look at their successes and feel genuinely inspired rather than diminished?

Imagine the liberation that would come from developing this capacity—the ability to witness someone's promotion, their beautiful relationship, their creative breakthrough, or their personal milestone and feel your heart expand with genuine joy for them rather than contract with self-doubt. What if you could train yourself to see their success not as evidence of your own shortcomings but as proof of what's possible in this world?

This isn't about forcing false positivity or pretending that initial pangs of comparison don't arise—they're deeply human responses that have been conditioned over years. Rather, it's about consciously cultivating a new neural pathway, one that leads toward inspiration instead of intimidation. What if you could learn to celebrate the success of others without it diminishing your own sense of worth or possibility?

Instead of habitually comparing yourself to others in that automatic, often painful way that we've all experienced, try consciously shifting your perspective toward genuinely celebrating their achievements. This isn't merely a surface-level adjustment in thinking—it's a fundamental rewiring of how you perceive success in the world around you. When you witness someone else's triumph, whether it's a colleague receiving recognition, a friend achieving a personal goal, or even a stranger sharing their accomplishment, take a deliberate moment to recognize that their success doesn't diminish, reduce, or take away from your own potential or worth—it actually serves as a powerful reminder and living proof that there's abundant room for everyone to succeed.

By consciously focusing your energy and attention on celebrating others rather than diminishing yourself through comparison, you begin to open yourself up to the profound and liberating idea that success doesn't have to operate as a limited resource, scarce and finite, where one person's gain inevitably means another's loss. This scarcity mindset, deeply ingrained in many of us from early childhood, suggests that achievements exist in a zero-sum game where opportunities are hoarded rather than shared.

But what if that fundamental assumption is wrong? What if there's actually plenty of room for everyone to shine, to flourish, and to achieve their own unique version of success? When you embrace this abundance mindset, you free yourself from the exhausting cycle of measuring your worth against others' accomplishments.

Reframe the entire way you view and approach comparison in your daily life. Instead of immediately falling into the familiar trap of thinking, "Why don't I have what they have?" or "Why haven't I achieved what they've accomplished?" try consciously shifting your internal dialogue to ask, "What can I learn from their journey?" or "What insights might their experience offer me?"

This seemingly simple mental adjustment requires practice and patience with yourself, but the transformation it creates can be truly remarkable. When you approach someone else's success with curiosity rather than envy, with openness rather than defensiveness, you transform what could have been a source of pain into an opportunity for growth and understanding.

You'll be genuinely surprised at how this fundamental shift in perspective can completely change not only the way you feel about yourself but also how you relate to and connect with others around you. Rather than viewing their achievements as evidence of your own inadequacy, you begin to see them as valuable teachers, as sources of inspiration, and as proof that the path you're walking has the potential to lead somewhere meaningful.

Final Thought: You Are on Your Own Path

The next time you find yourself slipping into that familiar pattern of measuring your life against someone else's carefully curated highlights, take a deep breath and gently remind yourself of this fundamental truth: You are exactly where you need to be at this precise moment in time. Your unique journey is unfolding at its own perfect pace, following rhythms and timelines that are entirely your own, and there is absolutely no universal deadline or prescribed schedule for what we call success.

The beauty of your path lies not in how quickly you reach certain milestones or how closely it mirrors someone else's trajectory, but in the authentic way it reflects your own values, circumstances, and growth. You already possess everything you need deep inside of you—the wisdom, the strength, the creativity, the resilience—to create and live a truly fulfilling, authentic life that aligns with who you are meant to be.

Don't allow the destructive habit of comparison to quietly steal away your joy, your inner peace, or your appreciation for the progress you've already made. Your story is still being written, and every chapter—including this one—has its own purpose and value.

You are not in competition with anyone else walking this earth—not your colleagues who seem to effortlessly climb the corporate ladder, not your friends who appear to have their relationships perfectly figured out, not the strangers on social media whose lives look impossibly polished and problem-free. This isn't a race where someone else's victory somehow diminishes your own potential for success and happiness.

The only person you truly need to be better than, the only meaningful comparison that will ever serve your growth and well-being, is the person you were yesterday—flawed, learning, doing the best you could with the knowledge and resources you had at that time.

In the next chapter that lies ahead, we'll delve deeply into the transformative importance of self-compassion—exploring how to treat yourself with the same gentle kindness, patience, and understanding you would naturally extend to a close friend who was struggling or facing challenges. We'll examine the ways in which self-compassion becomes a cornerstone of emotional healing, how it differs from self-pity or self-indulgence, and why it's such a crucial, foundational step in the ongoing journey toward genuine self-acceptance and inner peace.

This exploration of self-compassion will reveal practical techniques for quieting that harsh inner critic that so many of us carry, and I genuinely can't wait to share these insights and discoveries with you. But for this present moment, before we move forward, I want you to pause and take a few deep breaths to acknowledge your own inherent worth and value.

Right here, right now, exactly as you are—with all your perceived imperfections, your ongoing struggles, your unfinished goals, and your works in progress—you are enough. You are worthy of love, respect, and kindness, especially from yourself.

Chapter 4

The Power of Self-Compassion

What Is Self-Compassion?

Self-compassion is a deceptively simple yet profoundly powerful concept that can transform how we relate to ourselves during difficult moments. At its core, it's about treating yourself with the same genuine kindness, thoughtful care, and patient understanding that you would naturally offer to a close friend who was going through a hard time. It means extending to yourself the same warmth and empathy you'd show to someone you truly cared about.

When you find yourself struggling with life's inevitable challenges, facing setbacks that knock you off course, or dealing with the sting of failures and disappointments, take a moment to notice your internal response. Do you tend to unleash harsh criticism and beat yourself up mercilessly, replaying your mistakes over and over with brutal self-judgment? Or do you instinctively offer yourself the gentle encouragement, supportive words, and understanding that you need to heal and move forward?

If you're like the vast majority of people walking this earth, you're probably significantly harder on yourself than you would ever dream of being toward anyone else in your life. This tendency to show ourselves less compassion than we freely give to others is one of the most common yet overlooked sources of unnecessary suffering in our daily experience.

Many of us are remarkably quick to extend genuine compassion, understanding, and emotional support to others when they are navigating tough times, experiencing setbacks, or going through periods of struggle and pain. We naturally reach out with words of comfort, offering reassurance and perspective when friends, family members, or even strangers are facing difficulties. Yet when it comes to ourselves—when we're the ones stumbling, failing, or experiencing hardship—we transform into harsh critics, becoming judgmental, unforgiving, and mercilessly demanding.

We carry within us a deeply ingrained tendency to believe that to grow, improve, and become better versions of ourselves, we need to push ourselves relentlessly harder, criticize ourselves more severely, or wallow in feelings of guilt and shame about our inevitable mistakes and missteps. This internal narrative convinces us that self-punishment is somehow productive, that berating ourselves will motivate positive change, and that we must earn our way back to self-acceptance through perfect performance.

But authentic self-compassion isn't about letting yourself off the hook, avoiding personal responsibility, or making excuses for harmful behavior. Instead, it's about honestly acknowledging that you're human, just like everyone else walking this earth, complete with limitations, vulnerabilities, and the capacity for error. It's recognizing that you deserve the same fundamental compassion, patience, and understanding when things go wrong in your life as you would naturally offer to any other person facing similar challenges.

Why We Struggle with Self-Compassion

So why is it so incredibly difficult and emotionally challenging to practice genuine self-compassion in our daily lives? Why do we consistently find it so natural and effortless to be compassionate, understanding, and forgiving with others—extending grace to friends, family members, colleagues, and even complete strangers when they stumble or face adversity—but simultaneously find ourselves utterly incapable of showing ourselves even a fraction of that same kindness, patience, and gentle understanding when we're the ones who are struggling, hurting, or falling short of our own expectations?

A significant part of this struggle stems from deeply ingrained societal conditioning that permeates every aspect of our culture and upbringing. From our earliest childhood experiences through our educational systems and into our professional lives, we've been systematically taught and conditioned to believe that true success and worthiness are synonymous with absolute perfection. This cultural messaging bombards us constantly—through media representations, educational grading systems, workplace performance metrics, and social comparison dynamics that reinforce the notion that anything less than flawless execution represents fundamental failure.

Within this framework, mistakes aren't viewed as natural learning opportunities or inevitable parts of the human experience, but rather as glaring evidence of personal inadequacy and moral failing. This toxic belief system teaches us that failure—in any form, no matter how minor—means we are inherently not good enough, not smart enough, not capable enough to deserve success, love, or acceptance. We systematically internalize these harsh, unrealistic standards until they become the lens through which we evaluate every aspect of our performance and self-worth.

Consequently, we begin holding ourselves to these impossibly high, perfectionistic standards that no human being could realistically maintain. When we inevitably fall short of these unreachable expectations—as every person must—we automatically respond with harsh, relentless self-criticism and internal punishment. This self-flagellation only serves to deepen our feelings of inadequacy, shame, and fundamental unworthiness, creating a vicious cycle that becomes increasingly difficult to break free from.

Moreover, countless individuals among us carry within themselves an internal critic that operates with relentless intensity and unwavering persistence, delivering a constant barrage of harsh judgments and devastating assessments. This merciless inner voice maintains an endless stream of cruel commentary, repeatedly insisting that we are fundamentally inadequate, that we consistently fail to meet even the most basic standards, that we are destined to fall short of any meaningful achievement or success we might dare to pursue.

This deeply entrenched critical voice becomes so thoroughly woven into the fabric of our self-perception and identity that it essentially hijacks our internal dialogue, drowning out any possibility of gentleness or understanding toward ourselves. The critic's influence runs so profoundly deep that it fundamentally shapes and distorts how we interpret our experiences, evaluate our worth, and navigate our relationship with ourselves on the most basic level.

This internal adversary creates significant barriers to cultivating self-compassion because it has established such a powerful stronghold within our psychological landscape, making it extraordinarily challenging to extend the same kindness and understanding to ourselves that we would naturally offer to a dear friend facing similar struggles.

But here's the fundamental truth that cuts through all this internal criticism and self-doubt: You do not have to be perfect to deserve compassion.

This simple yet profound realization stands in direct opposition to everything that harsh inner critic has been telling you. It challenges the very foundation upon which your self-judgment operates. The compassion you deserve isn't something that must be earned through flawless performance, exceptional achievements, or meeting impossible standards. It isn't a reward that's withheld until you prove yourself worthy through perfection.

In fact, it's precisely your imperfections, your vulnerabilities, and your ongoing struggles that make you most deserving of self-compassion. These very human qualities—the mistakes you've made, the goals you haven't reached, the ways you've fallen short of your own expectations—are not disqualifications from compassion. They are, instead, the exact reasons why compassion is needed most urgently.

Everyone walking this earth has flaws that they wrestle with daily, makes mistakes that cause them regret, and faces difficulties that sometimes feel overwhelming—it's simply part of the shared human experience. These universal struggles don't make us broken or deficient; they make us human. Self-compassion isn't about turning a blind eye to your shortcomings or pretending your flaws don't exist; it's about treating yourself with genuine love, patience, and understanding precisely because of them, not despite them.

The Benefits of Self-Compassion

The transformative power of self-compassion lies in its remarkable ability to fundamentally reshape your emotional landscape, helping you build genuine emotional resilience that serves as an unshakable foundation during life's inevitable storms. This isn't merely about feeling better in the moment—it's about developing a deep, enduring capacity to weather difficulties with grace and return to a state of equilibrium more quickly when challenges arise.

When you consistently practice self-compassion, you're essentially rewiring your brain's response to stress and adversity. Instead of your nervous system going into overdrive at the first sign of trouble, you develop a more measured, thoughtful approach to handling life's pressures. This leads to a significant reduction in chronic stress levels, which in turn has cascading positive effects on both your mental and physical health.

Extensive psychological research has consistently demonstrated that individuals who cultivate self-compassion experience profoundly different outcomes when facing life's inevitable setbacks. They're not only more likely to bounce back from disappointments, failures, and traumatic experiences, but they also report feeling genuinely better about themselves throughout the recovery process. Rather than getting trapped in cycles of self-recrimination and despair, they're able to maintain perspective and move through difficult emotions with remarkable resilience.

Perhaps most importantly, those who practice self-compassion develop an enhanced ability to handle stress more effectively in real time. They recover from perceived failures and actual mistakes with considerably more grace and dignity, maintaining a healthier, more balanced sense of self-worth that isn't contingent on external validation or perfect performance.

Self-compassion also has a profoundly transformative impact on your overall mental health and emotional well-being. It creates a powerful buffer against the destructive forces of anxiety, depression, and shame that can so easily overwhelm us during difficult times. When you consistently practice treating yourself with genuine kindness and understanding, you're fundamentally less likely to spiral down into those familiar, destructive negative thinking patterns that once seemed inescapable.

Instead of allowing yourself to feel completely defeated and worthless when you inevitably make mistakes or face setbacks, you gradually learn to reframe these experiences entirely. You begin to view your errors, missteps, and failures not as evidence of your inadequacy or proof that you're fundamentally flawed, but rather as valuable opportunities for meaningful growth, deeper learning, and genuine personal development.

This shift in perspective doesn't happen overnight, but with consistent practice, it becomes increasingly natural. You start to approach your own struggles with the same gentle curiosity and patient understanding that you would naturally extend to someone you care about deeply.

When you finally stop the relentless cycle of beating yourself up over every perceived misstep and shortcoming, you fundamentally open the door to genuine personal growth and deep, lasting healing. This shift creates a profound transformation in how you relate to yourself and your experiences. You begin to give yourself the precious mental and emotional space necessary to truly learn from your experiences without the harsh, punitive judgment that once clouded every reflection.

This newfound breathing room allows your mind to process events more clearly and objectively. Instead of immediately jumping to self-criticism and blame, you can examine what happened with curiosity and understanding. You can ask yourself what lessons might be hidden within the difficulty, what wisdom you might extract from the pain, and how you might approach similar situations differently in the future.

This gentler, more compassionate approach to self-reflection creates a foundation from which you can move forward with significantly greater confidence and genuine peace of mind. You're no longer carrying the heavy burden of constant self-recrimination, which frees up enormous amounts of mental and emotional energy that can be redirected toward positive growth and meaningful change.

Exercise: Write Yourself a Compassionate Letter

Now that you have gained a deeper understanding of the transformative power of self-compassion and how it can fundamentally reshape your relationship with yourself, it's time to transition from theory to practical application. The journey from intellectual understanding to embodied practice requires intentional steps and concrete exercises that help you begin to genuinely show yourself the same warmth, understanding, and unconditional kindness that you would naturally and instinctively offer to a dear friend who is struggling.

This shift from self-criticism to self-compassion doesn't happen overnight—it's a gradual process that requires patience, practice, and gentle persistence. The following exercise serves as a powerful starting point, offering you a tangible way to begin cultivating this new relationship with yourself.

Take a moment to pause and think deeply about a recent struggle or difficult situation you've faced in your life. This could be a significant mistake you made at work or in a relationship, a personal challenge you've been avoiding or putting off, a decision you're second-guessing, or perhaps an ongoing situation that has been causing you considerable stress and anxiety. Allow yourself to really sit with this experience for a moment, acknowledging the emotions that arise as you reflect on it.

Now shift your perspective entirely and imagine that your very best friend—someone you care about deeply and unconditionally—is going through something remarkably similar to what you're experiencing. Picture them sitting across from you, their face reflecting the same worry, disappointment, or frustration that you've been carrying. What would your natural, instinctive response be? What words of support, encouragement, and understanding would flow naturally from your heart? How would you speak to them about their situation, and what tone would you use to convey your care and belief in their ability to navigate through this difficult time?

Now take this exercise one step further and write a heartfelt letter to yourself, approaching it with the exact same warmth, compassion, and understanding that you would naturally extend to a cherished friend who's experiencing the very same difficulties and challenges. Be genuinely kind and gentle with yourself in your words, demonstrating the same level of understanding and empathy that you would offer without hesitation to someone you love deeply.

Acknowledge and validate the real struggles you're facing—don't minimize them or brush them aside—but also take the time to lovingly remind yourself of your inherent worth as a person, your proven inner strength that has carried you through previous hardships, and your remarkable ability to overcome difficulties and emerge stronger. Write to yourself as if you were speaking to someone you believe in wholeheartedly, someone whose potential you see clearly even when they cannot see it themselves.

Here's an example of what a self-compassionate letter might look like:

> Dear Me,
>
> I know you've been carrying such a heavy weight lately, feeling overwhelmed and perhaps questioning yourself at every turn. I want you to know that it's completely okay to feel this way—these emotions are valid, and you don't need to apologize for experiencing them. Life has thrown some particularly challenging circumstances your way recently, and anyone in your position would be struggling with similar feelings of uncertainty and doubt.
>
> I need you to understand something important: Everyone makes mistakes, faces set-

backs, and encounters obstacles that feel insurmountable at times. These experiences, difficult as they are, don't diminish your worth as a person or erase the countless positive qualities that make you who you are. You're still deserving of love and respect, you're still inherently valuable just as you are, and you possess far more strength and resilience than you're giving yourself credit for right now.

When I look at your journey, I see someone who has weathered storms before and emerged with wisdom and grace. I'm genuinely proud of you for how far you've traveled, for the courage you've shown in facing your fears, and for the persistence you've demonstrated even when the path ahead seemed unclear. I know that right now each step forward might feel exhausting and slow, but please remember that progress doesn't always announce itself with fanfare—sometimes it whispers in small, quiet moments of growth.

You don't have to be perfect, and you never did. All I ask is that you continue being gentle with yourself as you navigate this chapter of your life, treating yourself with the same kindness you would offer a dear friend facing similar struggles.

With endless love and unwavering belief in you,

—Yourself

Cultivating Self-Compassion Daily

Self-compassion isn't something you practice once and forget about—it's an ongoing, ever-evolving process that requires patience, dedication, and gentle persistence as you cultivate it every single day. Like tending to a delicate garden that needs consistent care and attention, self-compassion grows stronger with regular nurturing and mindful cultivation. It's a skill that deepens over time, becoming more natural and instinctive the more you commit to practicing it with intention and care.

The beautiful truth is that self-compassion can be woven seamlessly into the fabric of your everyday life through small meaningful gestures and mindful moments of kindness toward yourself. You don't need to set aside hours or completely restructure your routine—instead, you can discover countless opportunities throughout each day to treat yourself with the same gentleness and understanding you would offer to someone you deeply care about. Here are a few simple, practical ways to thoughtfully integrate self-compassion into your daily routine, creating a foundation of self-love that will support you through both ordinary moments and challenging times:

Final Thought: You Deserve Love, Especially from Yourself

It's time to stop waiting for others to give you the love and compassion that you can give yourself right now, in this very moment. You don't need to earn it through achievements or accolades. You don't need to be perfect, flawless, or have all the answers. You don't need to prove your worthiness through endless accomplishments or by meeting impossible standards that shift every time you get close to reaching them.

You deserve love and kindness simply because you're human—because you have a beating heart, because you feel deeply, because you're trying your best to navigate this complex world with all its challenges and uncertainties. Your humanity itself is your qualification for compassion. The fact that you wake up each day and continue moving forward, despite whatever struggles you may be facing, is reason enough to treat yourself with tenderness and understanding.

The more you practice self-compassion—day after day, moment after moment—the more profound changes you'll begin to notice rippling through every aspect of your life. You'll start to believe in your own inherent worth and remarkable resilience in ways that might surprise you. This isn't just positive thinking or wishful optimism; it's a fundamental rewiring of how you relate to yourself and your experiences.

You'll find yourself naturally stopping the harsh internal dialogue that once felt so automatic and necessary. Instead of seeing mistakes as devastating failures that define your character or predict your future, you'll gradually begin to recognize them for what they truly are: valuable opportunities for learning, growth, and deeper self-understanding. Each misstep becomes a teacher rather than a tormentor, each setback a chance to practice bouncing back with greater wisdom and grace.

As this shift deepens, you'll discover that you're becoming genuinely kinder to yourself—not in a superficial way, but with the same warmth and understanding you'd naturally offer a dear friend going through similar struggles. You'll develop more patience with your own progress, understanding that meaningful change takes time and that growth rarely follows a straight line. Most importantly, you'll become more forgiving when you inevitably fall short of your own expectations, recognizing that this too is part of the beautifully imperfect human experience.

In the next chapter, we'll embark on a profound exploration of how discovering your true purpose can serve as a powerful catalyst for embracing the magnificent, complex, and entirely unique person you were always meant to be. We'll delve into the transformative process of understanding what truly matters to you at the deepest level—those core values, passions, and callings that make your heart sing and your spirit come alive. This understanding will become the foundation that empowers you to craft and live a life that authentically reflects your genuine self, rather than the version of yourself you think others expect you to be.

We'll examine how purpose acts as both compass and anchor, guiding your decisions while keeping you grounded in what feels most true and meaningful to you. You'll learn to distinguish between the shoulds and musts imposed by external expectations and the gentle, persistent whispers of your own inner wisdom that point toward your authentic path.

But for now, in this quiet moment between chapters, take a slow, deep breath that fills your entire being with calm awareness. Let the air settle into your lungs as you pause to offer yourself this simple yet profound reminder: You are enough, exactly as you are—not when you achieve more, not when you fix what you perceive as broken, not when you finally become the person you think you should be. Right here, right now, in all your beautiful imperfection and work-in-progress humanity, you are completely, utterly, and unconditionally enough.

Chapter 5

Discovering Your Purpose

The Quest for Purpose

Have you ever found yourself lying awake at night, staring at the ceiling with an inexplicable feeling that something fundamental was missing from your life? That nagging sensation that you were simply drifting through your days, going through the familiar motions of work, relationships, and responsibilities, yet feeling strangely disconnected from any real sense of direction or deep fulfillment?

Perhaps you've caught yourself in quiet moments—during your morning commute, while washing dishes, or in the brief pause between tasks—when that persistent thought suddenly surfaces with startling clarity: There has to be more to life than this. The feeling might wash over you like a gentle wave or hit you with the force of a revelation, leaving you questioning not just what you're doing but why you're doing it.

This profound sense of searching, this restless yearning for something more meaningful, is a feeling that countless people experience throughout their lives. It doesn't discriminate based on age, career success, or life circumstances. You might encounter it in your twenties when you're first establishing your path, in your forties during a midlife reassessment, or even in your later years when you're reflecting on your legacy. These moments of existential questioning aren't signs of failure or weakness—they're completely natural human experiences that signal your deeper need for purpose and meaning.

But what if I told you that your purpose doesn't need to be a grand, earth-shattering revelation that transforms everything overnight? What if instead of waiting for some dramatic moment of clarity to strike like lightning, it's something you can begin uncovering right now, today, in small but deeply intentional ways? What if the very search itself—this gentle exploration of who you are and what matters to you—is already part of the journey toward fulfillment?

The truth is, purpose isn't always something you're born instinctively knowing, like some predetermined destiny written in the stars. It's not a hidden treasure map that you either possess or don't. Rather, it's something far more organic and evolving—something you gradually discover and nurture over time through your genuine passions, your accumulated experiences both joyful and challenging, and the unique ways you naturally connect with and respond to the world around you.

This discovery unfolds through the quiet moments when you notice what energizes you, through the conversations that leave you feeling truly alive, and through the activities that make you lose track of time. It emerges when you pay attention to what breaks your heart about the world's problems, what sparks your curiosity, and what brings you a sense of deep satisfaction that goes beyond mere accomplishment.

The process of discovering your purpose is deeply personal and uniquely yours. It's not a one-size-fits-all formula that can be packaged neatly into universal steps or guidelines. What brings one person profound joy and fulfillment—whether it's teaching children, building businesses, creating art, or caring for others—might not resonate with you at all, and that's not only okay, it's exactly as it should be. Your purpose is as individual as your fingerprint, shaped by your particular blend of experiences, talents, perspectives, and the specific way you see and interact with the world.

But here's the beautiful truth that emerges when you begin to honor this personal journey: When you gradually align your daily actions, choices, and commitments with your emerging sense of purpose, something profound shifts within you. You start to feel a deeper, more sustained sense of meaning that goes beyond fleeting happiness or temporary satisfaction. It's not just about feeling good in the moment—it's about feeling deeply connected to something larger than yourself, something that gives weight and significance to your everyday experiences.

As this alignment deepens, you begin to understand your unique role in the intricate tapestry of the world around you. This knowledge becomes like an internal compass, quietly but consistently guiding you through life's complexities with a renewed sense of direction and clear intention. Decisions become easier because you have a framework for what truly matters, and even ordinary moments take on new significance when viewed through the lens of your purpose.

Understanding What Purpose Really Means

Purpose doesn't always have to be something monumental, earth-shattering, or career-defining that appears in newspaper headlines or history books. It can simply mean living in thoughtful alignment with your deeply held values and authentic passions, allowing these guiding principles to inform the choices you make each day. Sometimes the smallest, most seemingly insignificant actions—a gentle word of encouragement to a struggling colleague, taking time to truly listen to a friend in need, or simply approaching your daily responsibilities with genuine care and attention—can bring the most profound and lasting sense of purpose to your life.

The beauty lies in recognizing that purpose often manifests not in grand gestures or dramatic life changes but in the quiet consistency of small meaningful acts that reflect who you truly are at your core. These moments of authentic living create ripples of meaning that extend far beyond what you might initially perceive, touching lives and creating connections in ways you may never fully realize.

For example, maybe your purpose is to gently spread kindness and compassion to everyone you encounter in your daily journey, offering warm smiles to strangers, patient understanding to those who frustrate you, and genuine empathy to those who cross your path. Or perhaps it's to inspire and uplift others through your unique creative expression—whether that's through art, writing, music, cooking, or simply the innovative way you approach problem-solving in your everyday work and relationships.

Your purpose might be to serve as a steadfast, supportive friend who creates a safe harbor for others during life's inevitable storms, someone who listens without judgment and offers comfort when words fail. It could be to embody the role of a loving, nurturing partner who brings out the best in your significant other while growing together through shared experiences and mutual respect. Maybe your calling is to become a passionate advocate for a cause that ignites your soul—environmental protection, social justice, education, animal welfare, or community development—using your voice and actions to create positive change in whatever capacity feels authentic to you.

The profound truth is that purpose doesn't have to manifest as a huge, publicly visible contribution that garners recognition or accolades from the wider world. It can simply be the quiet, consistent practice of living authentically and intentionally within your own unique circumstances, honoring your values through your choices, and allowing your genuine self to shine through in every interaction and decision you make.

How to Begin Discovering Your Purpose

The journey to discovering your authentic purpose often begins with the essential step of developing a deeper understanding of your core passions, fundamental values, and natural strengths. This process of self-discovery requires patience and honest introspection, as it involves peeling back the layers of external expectations and societal conditioning to reveal what truly resonates with your soul.

Finding your purpose isn't about forcing an immediate revelation or expecting a dramatic epiphany to strike like lightning. Instead, it's about creating space for quiet reflection and gentle exploration of the patterns and themes that have woven themselves throughout your life experiences. Here are several thoughtful questions you can ask yourself to help gradually uncover and illuminate what truly matters to you at the deepest level:

Exercise: Discover Your Passion

Take some time to reflect on the following:

Living in Alignment with Your Purpose

Once you begin to uncover your passions, values, and strengths, the next crucial step is to thoughtfully align your daily life with these fundamental aspects of who you are. This transformative process means making deliberate, intentional choices that authentically reflect what matters most deeply to you at your core. It's about embracing the courage to live genuinely and authentically, refusing to simply go through the motions of existence or blindly following someone else's predetermined expectations, societal pressures, or prescribed blueprint for what your life should look like.

True alignment requires honest self-reflection and the willingness to make changes, both large and small, that bring your external circumstances into harmony with your internal compass. This might mean reassessing relationships that no longer serve your growth, reconsidering career paths that feel misaligned with your values, or simply adjusting daily habits and routines to better support your authentic self. The goal isn't perfection, but rather a conscious ongoing effort to live with greater integrity and purpose, ensuring that your actions consistently reflect the person you genuinely are and aspire to become.

Living in alignment with your purpose also involves cultivating a mindset of openness and receptivity to the natural ebb and flow of change and personal growth that characterizes the human experience. As you continue to evolve, mature, and gain new experiences throughout different seasons of your life, so too will your understanding of what truly brings you deep fulfillment and genuine satisfaction. Your sense of purpose may shift, expand, and grow alongside you as you encounter new challenges, relationships, and opportunities that reshape your perspective and broaden your understanding of yourself and the world around you.

This evolution is not only natural but also necessary for authentic living. What resonated deeply with you in your twenties may feel less compelling in your forties, and the causes that stirred your passion as a young adult might give way to different concerns and interests as you gain wisdom and life experience. Rather than viewing these changes as inconsistencies or failures, embrace them as signs of healthy growth and deeper self-awareness.

Purpose isn't a fixed destination that you arrive at once and remain static within forever—it's an ongoing, dynamic journey of discovery and rediscovery, one that continues to unfold, surprise, and guide you as you live fully, learn continuously, and remain open to the endless possibilities that life presents along the way.

Exercise: Create a Purpose Statement

A great way to keep yourself grounded in your evolving sense of purpose is to create a personal purpose statement—a concise meaningful declaration that captures the essence of what drives you and gives your life direction. This carefully crafted statement can serve as a powerful anchor and compass, providing a reminder of what you want to focus on in your life and how you want to show up and live each day with intention and authenticity.

Think of your purpose statement as a living document that reflects your core values, deepest aspirations, and the unique contribution you want to make to the world around you. Unlike rigid mission statements that corporations might develop, your personal purpose statement should feel organic, inspiring, and true to who you are at your core. It should resonate with your heart and mind, capturing both your current understanding of what matters most to you while remaining flexible enough to evolve as you continue to grow and change throughout your life's journey.

To create your own purpose statement, consider the following:

Once you've thought through these questions, combine your answers into a simple statement. For example:

Write this statement down and keep it somewhere visible. Whenever you feel lost or uncertain, return to it as a reminder of what truly matters to you.

Final Thought: Purpose Is in the Present Moment

While it's tempting to think of purpose as some grand destination we're supposed to "discover" somewhere out there in the distant future—perhaps through a dramatic revelation or life-changing event—the truth is far more immediate and accessible than that. Your purpose isn't hiding in some far-off tomorrow, waiting to be unearthed through years of searching or soul-searching journeys to exotic places. Instead, it's continuously revealing itself and unfolding in the present moment, woven into the fabric of your everyday experiences and decisions.

Each choice you make throughout your day, no matter how seemingly small or insignificant, carries the potential to align you more closely with your authentic self. Whether it's choosing to speak up for someone who's being treated unfairly, deciding to pursue a creative project that excites you, or simply responding to a friend's text with genuine care and attention, these moments all contribute to the ongoing expression of who you truly are.

Each action you take, each word you speak, each gesture of kindness or act of courage can serve as a stepping stone that brings you incrementally closer to living a life that genuinely reflects your deepest values, your natural talents, and the unique contribution you're here to make. Your purpose isn't something you need to wait to stumble upon—it's something you can actively embody and express right now, in this very moment, through the conscious choices you make and the authentic way you show up in the world.

Remember, purpose isn't about having everything figured out or possessing some grand master plan that dictates every step of your journey. It's not about achieving some mythical state of complete clarity where all uncertainty vanishes and your path becomes crystal clear. Instead, it's about living authentically in each moment, genuinely engaging with your passions and interests as they arise, and consistently staying true to your core values even when the world around you seems to be pulling in different directions.

The more you consciously align your daily actions and decisions with what feels genuinely right to you—what resonates with your inner wisdom and speaks to your heart—the more your unique purpose will naturally begin to emerge and become clear. This clarity doesn't arrive all at once like a lightning bolt of revelation, but rather unfolds gradually, like a flower blooming petal by petal, as you continue to honor your authentic self in both small everyday moments and significant life choices.

In the next chapter, we'll delve deeply into how surrounding yourself with positive, uplifting energy and cultivating relationships with the right kinds of people—those who truly see and appreciate your authentic self—can provide invaluable support and encouragement for your ongoing journey toward living with genuine authenticity and purpose.

But for this moment, right here and now, I want you to hold onto this fundamental truth: Your purpose isn't something distant or external that you need to search for in far-off places or exotic experiences. It isn't hidden in some remote corner of the world waiting to be discovered through grand adventures or spiritual pilgrimages. Rather, your purpose is intimately woven into the very fabric of who you are—it lives within the depths of your being, nestled in your heart, mind, and soul.

You don't need to look outside yourself, scanning the horizon for signs or waiting for others to validate your path. Your purpose is already there, patiently residing within you like a seed that contains all the potential for growth and flowering. It's waiting quietly for you to slow down, turn inward, and begin the gentle, loving process of uncovering and nurturing what has always been yours to claim.

Chapter 6

Surrounding Yourself with Positive Energy

The Influence of People Around You

Have you ever walked into a room and immediately felt the atmosphere shift around you—either positively or negatively? It's one of those unmistakable sensations that hits you before you even fully understand what's happening. The air seems to change, your shoulders either relax or tense up, and something deep within your gut tells you whether this space feels safe or threatening.

Maybe you've been fortunate enough to be around people who genuinely uplift you, those rare individuals who make you feel truly motivated, deeply seen, and authentically heard. These are the people who notice when you've achieved something meaningful, who remember the small details about your life that matter to you, and who somehow manage to make you feel like the best version of yourself simply by being in their presence.

On the other hand, perhaps you've also spent considerable time with people who leave you feeling completely drained, unexpectedly anxious, or fundamentally unworthy. These interactions might start innocently enough, but by the end of your time together, you find yourself questioning your choices, doubting your abilities, or feeling an overwhelming sense of exhaustion that seems to seep into your bones.

The fundamental truth is that the people you consciously choose to surround yourself with—and those you unconsciously allow into your inner circle—have an incredibly profound and lasting effect on virtually every aspect of your life. They don't just casually influence your daily mindset or temporarily shift your energy levels; they actively shape your core beliefs about yourself, your capabilities, your worthiness, and your place in the world. These individuals become the invisible architects of your self-perception, gradually molding how you view your potential and limitations.

We've all heard the widely quoted saying, "You are the average of the five people you spend the most time with," and while it might sound like oversimplified wisdom at first glance, there's actually a tremendous amount of psychological truth embedded within those words. The people you regularly interact with—whether they're family members, close friends, romantic partners, colleagues, or even casual acquaintances—continuously shape and reshape how you fundamentally see yourself and how you instinctively approach the complexities of the world around you.

Their words become the internal voice that either encourages or discourages you when you're facing challenges. Their reactions to your dreams and aspirations either fuel your confidence or plant seeds of doubt that can grow into limiting beliefs. Even their unspoken attitudes and energy can seep into your subconscious, gradually altering your own emotional baseline and influencing the lens through which you interpret your experiences and possibilities.

Positive energy is genuinely contagious in the most beautiful and transformative way. When you consistently surround yourself with people who not only support your journey but actively celebrate your uniqueness, champion your dreams, and encourage your authentic growth at every turn, you naturally begin to feel more confident, empowered, and secure in your journey toward becoming your truest self. These supportive relationships create a protective bubble of encouragement that allows you to take risks, explore new aspects of yourself, and push beyond your comfort zone without fear of harsh judgment.

On the other hand, negative energy—whether it manifests through toxic relationships that drain your spirit, jealousy that makes others diminish your achievements, persistent criticism that chips away at your self-worth, or subtle undermining that plants seeds of self-doubt—can gradually pull you down into a darker headspace and significantly hinder your personal growth. This negativity acts like an invisible weight, making every step forward feel more difficult and causing you to question your own instincts and worthiness along the way.

This chapter is all about gaining a deep and comprehensive understanding of the profound impact that your immediate environment—both physical and emotional—has on your personal development, and then taking deliberate, intentional steps to carefully curate and surround yourself with the specific types of people, relationships, and positive energy sources that will genuinely nourish, support, and encourage the authentic expression of your true self.

Recognizing Positive Energy

Positive energy manifests itself in countless different forms and expressions throughout our daily lives. It's not simply about surrounding yourself with people who maintain an artificially cheerful demeanor or relentlessly optimistic outlook at every moment; rather, it's about cultivating relationships with individuals who consistently lift you up, validate your worth, and make you feel genuinely good about who you are at your core, exactly as you are in this very moment, without requiring you to change or mask any part of your authentic self.

This type of positive energy can be discovered and recognized in those special individuals who naturally embody certain key characteristics and behaviors. These are the people who seem to radiate a warm, supportive presence that draws you in and makes you feel both comfortable and inspired. Positive energy can be found in those who:

Positive people possess an almost magical ability to help you feel genuinely inspired, deeply motivated, and powerfully connected to your authentic purpose in life. They serve as beacons of encouragement during your darkest moments, consistently offering unwavering support and gentle guidance that helps illuminate your path forward. These remarkable individuals have a natural gift for seeing your potential even when you've lost sight of it yourself, and they remind you of your inherent worth and capabilities through both their words and actions.

When life becomes overwhelming and obstacles seem insurmountable, these positive influences encourage you to keep pushing forward, offering both practical wisdom and emotional sustenance that helps you navigate through challenging times. They celebrate your victories, no matter how small, and help you reframe setbacks as learning opportunities rather than failures. Their presence in your life creates a ripple effect of optimism that strengthens your resilience and renews your determination.

Most importantly, they make you genuinely believe in your untapped potential and remind you that your dreams are not only valid but achievable with persistence and dedication.

The Effects of Negative Energy

On the flip side, negative energy can have a much more subtle yet profoundly damaging effect on your life, seeping into your consciousness like a slow poison that gradually weakens your spirit. It's remarkably easy to ignore or overlook how toxic people or environments can slowly but systematically drain your precious energy, undermine your hard-earned confidence, and chip away at your fundamental sense of self-worth and identity. The insidious nature of this negativity makes it particularly dangerous because it often operates below the radar of conscious awareness, making its destructive impact feel almost invisible until significant damage has already been done.

When you're constantly surrounded by negativity—whether through pessimistic conversations, critical remarks, or an atmosphere of perpetual complaint and dissatisfaction—it can begin to erode your self-esteem in ways that feel both gradual and inevitable. This toxic environment creates a mental fog that clouds your judgment and makes it increasingly difficult to maintain perspective on your own value and capabilities. The negative energy acts like emotional quicksand, slowly pulling you down into patterns of self-doubt and limiting beliefs that can take considerable time and effort to overcome.

Toxic relationships, whether they develop with family members who should be sources of support, friends who were once trusted confidants, or colleagues in your professional environment, can manifest themselves in numerous destructive and often subtle ways that gradually undermine your well-being:

When you find yourself consistently surrounded by this kind of toxic, draining energy, it becomes alarmingly easy to begin questioning every aspect of yourself, doubting your inherent worth and value as a person, and feeling increasingly disconnected from your authentic self and the core values that once guided your decisions with clarity and confidence. The constant exposure to negativity, manipulation, and emotional depletion creates a fog of confusion that clouds your judgment and makes it difficult to distinguish between your genuine thoughts and feelings and the distorted perceptions that have been gradually imposed upon you through these harmful interactions.

This disconnection from your true self can manifest in various ways—you might find yourself making choices that feel foreign to your nature, agreeing to things that contradict your values, or simply feeling lost and uncertain about who you really are beneath the layers of doubt and self-criticism that have accumulated over time. The more you're exposed to these energy-draining relationships, the more your internal compass becomes unreliable, leaving you feeling adrift and struggling to reconnect with the authentic version of yourself that exists beneath the surface of accumulated negativity and self-doubt.

Identifying and Setting Boundaries

One of the most crucial and transformative aspects of surrounding yourself with positive, uplifting energy is the deliberate and thoughtful practice of setting clear, firm boundaries in all areas of your life. These boundaries serve as essential protective barriers that are absolutely fundamental for maintaining healthy, balanced relationships and safeguarding your precious emotional well-being from the constant bombardment of negativity and toxicity that can so easily seep into your daily experiences.

Boundaries function as powerful tools that help you clearly define and establish what constitutes acceptable behavior from others and what absolutely isn't tolerable in your personal space and relationships. They act as invisible but vital lines of demarcation that protect your energy, your peace of mind, and your sense of self-worth. More importantly, well-established boundaries ensure that you consistently prioritize your own legitimate needs, core values, and emotional health without feeling guilty or selfish for doing so.

When you fail to establish these protective boundaries, you inadvertently leave yourself vulnerable to the very energy vampires and toxic influences that can gradually erode your confidence and sense of self. Setting boundaries isn't about building walls or shutting people out entirely; rather, it's about creating healthy parameters that allow positive relationships to flourish while filtering out the harmful dynamics that threaten to undermine your progress and well-being.

If you find yourself constantly feeling emotionally drained, mentally exhausted, or perpetually unappreciated after interactions with someone in your life, it's a clear signal that the time has come to seriously reassess the dynamics of that relationship and establish much clearer, more defined boundaries. This process of boundary-setting can prove to be exceptionally difficult and emotionally challenging, particularly when the person in question is someone who occupies a significant place in your life—whether it's a family member, a long-time friend, a romantic partner, or even a colleague you see daily. The emotional complexity of these situations often makes us hesitate, second-guess ourselves, or feel guilty about the very idea of creating distance or limitations.

However, despite the discomfort and potential resistance you might encounter, setting these protective boundaries is absolutely necessary and nonnegotiable for your continued personal growth, emotional development, and overall happiness. Without these essential safeguards in place, you risk allowing toxic patterns to continue unchecked, potentially sabotaging your progress and undermining your self-worth in the process.

Here are some practical, actionable tips for establishing and maintaining healthy boundaries that will serve you well:

By consciously and deliberately setting these protective boundaries, you actively reclaim control over the emotional and psychological energy you permit to enter and influence your daily existence. You create a powerful shield that guards against the insidious effects of toxicity, negativity, and draining interactions that can slowly erode your sense of self-worth and inner peace.

In doing so, you simultaneously cultivate and nurture a sacred space within your life—a sanctuary where positivity, growth, and authentic self-expression can naturally flourish and flow freely, unimpeded by the harsh judgment, manipulation, or energy-depleting behaviors that may have previously dominated your relationships and daily interactions.

Surrounding Yourself with Supportive People

As much as it's critically important to establish and maintain firm boundaries with negative influences and toxic personalities, it's equally essential—if not more so—to consciously and intentionally surround yourself with people who genuinely support, encourage, and believe in you. These are the precious individuals who consistently uplift your spirit and wholeheartedly encourage you to embrace and express your most authentic self without fear or reservation.

They are the ones who celebrate your achievements with genuine enthusiasm and joy, no matter how big or small those victories might seem to the outside world. Whether you've landed your dream job, overcome a personal challenge, learned a new skill, or simply made it through a particularly difficult day, these supportive souls recognize the significance of your progress and make it a point to acknowledge your efforts and accomplishments.

More importantly, these remarkable people serve as gentle yet powerful reminders of your inherent worth and value, especially during those inevitable moments when self-doubt creeps in and you begin to forget your own strength and capabilities. They see your potential even when you can't see it yourself, and they possess the wisdom and compassion to reflect back to you the beautiful qualities that make you uniquely valuable.

Here are some thoughtful and practical ways to actively cultivate and nurture these supportive, life-affirming relationships:

Surrounding yourself with genuinely supportive, positive people doesn't mean you'll suddenly have perfect relationships free from all conflict, misunderstanding, or challenging moments, but it does mean that you'll have cultivated a meaningful network of individuals who consistently help you grow, learn from your experiences, overcome obstacles with grace, and become the most authentic, confident, and fulfilled version of yourself through their encouragement, wisdom, and unwavering belief in your potential.

Exercise: Create Your Circle of Support

Take some time to reflect deeply and thoughtfully on the people who currently populate your life, considering both your immediate circle and your broader network of relationships. Find a quiet, comfortable space where you can think without distraction, and write down the specific names of individuals who consistently lift you up emotionally, mentally, and spiritually, making you feel genuinely supported, valued, and appreciated for exactly who you are.

These are the precious people who wholeheartedly celebrate your authentic self, your unique qualities, your accomplishments both big and small, and who actively encourage your personal growth and evolution without trying to change or diminish you. They demonstrate genuine kindness, show you consistent respect for your thoughts and feelings, honor your boundaries, and create a safe emotional space where you feel comfortable being vulnerable and expressing your true thoughts and emotions without fear of judgment or criticism.

Next, shift your focus to examine those relationships that consistently leave you feeling emotionally drained, mentally exhausted, or somehow diminished in your sense of self-worth and confidence. Take time to honestly identify the specific individuals who make you feel small, insignificant, or less than your authentic self when you're in their presence or after interacting with them.

Write down in detail how these particular relationships impact your emotional well-being, your mental state, and your overall energy levels. Consider the subtle ways they might undermine your confidence, dismiss your feelings, or make you question your own worth and validity. Reflect on whether these interactions leave you feeling confused, anxious, or emotionally depleted long after the encounter has ended.

As you examine these dynamics, consider what specific boundaries you need to establish moving forward to protect your emotional well-being and preserve your precious energy. Ask yourself honestly: Are there relationships in your life that need to fundamentally change, be completely redefined with new parameters and expectations, or perhaps even be gracefully released altogether for the sake of your mental health and personal growth?

Final Thought: Your Energy Is Precious

Remember, the energy you surround yourself with serves as a direct mirror, reflecting not only how you perceive your own worth and value but also the standards you've set for how others are permitted to treat you. This energy becomes the invisible force that either elevates your spirit or slowly erodes your sense of self, making it one of the most crucial elements in your journey toward authentic living.

Make a conscious, deliberate choice to surround yourself with people who genuinely inspire you to reach higher, who motivate you to pursue your dreams with unwavering determination, and who respect the entirety of who you are—your strengths, your vulnerabilities, your quirks, and your authentic essence. These are the individuals who see your potential even when you struggle to see it yourself, who celebrate your victories without jealousy, and who offer genuine support during your moments of doubt or difficulty.

Simultaneously, give yourself the profound gift of releasing those relationships that consistently leave you feeling emotionally depleted, mentally exhausted, or somehow less than your true self. This isn't about harboring resentment or bitterness; it's about recognizing that not every relationship is meant to last forever, and that some connections may have served their purpose in your life's journey. Grant yourself the liberating permission to prioritize your emotional well-being and mental health above the obligation to maintain relationships that no longer serve your highest good.

The journey to authenticity is not merely about shifting your internal perspective or transforming how you perceive yourself; it encompasses the far more comprehensive task of deliberately creating and cultivating an environment that actively nurtures your personal growth and supports your evolution into your most genuine self. This process requires both internal work and external awareness, demanding that you become increasingly mindful of the energetic atmosphere you inhabit daily.

When you make the intentional decision to create space for positive energy in your life—whether through the relationships you maintain, the conversations you engage in, or the environments you choose to frequent—you are essentially constructing a sanctuary where your true self can not only survive but genuinely flourish. This nurturing environment becomes a fertile ground where your authentic thoughts can take root, where your genuine emotions can be expressed without fear of judgment, and where your real dreams and aspirations can grow without the suffocating weight of negativity or toxic influences that might otherwise stunt their development.

In the upcoming chapter that follows, we will delve deeply into the transformative process of how living your fundamental truth can evolve into a consistent, meaningful daily practice—exploring the nuanced ways to wholeheartedly embrace and embody authenticity in every single aspect and dimension of your multifaceted life. We'll examine practical strategies for weaving genuine self-expression into your everyday interactions, decision-making processes, and personal choices.

But for this present moment, take a slow, deliberate, and deeply nourishing breath that fills your lungs completely. Allow yourself the time and space to honestly assess and evaluate the intimate circle of people who surround you on a regular basis. Consider the quality of energy they bring into your world, the conversations they inspire, and the feelings they evoke within you.

Above all, hold this essential truth close to your heart and remember it with unwavering conviction: You absolutely deserve to be surrounded by positive, genuinely supportive, and uplifting energy in every corner of your life. You are worthy of relationships that celebrate your growth, conversations that inspire your spirit, and connections that honor the beautiful, authentic person you are becoming.

Chapter 7

Living Your Truth

The Power of Authenticity

Living your truth is fundamentally about being genuine and honest with yourself in every facet of your existence. It's about creating a deep, meaningful alignment between your innermost thoughts, your daily actions, and the decisions you make with your core values, your burning passions, and the authentic essence of who you truly are at your very foundation. This isn't merely about occasional moments of honesty or sporadic bursts of self-expression. Authenticity isn't just a single momentous choice you make once and then forget about. Rather, it's an ongoing, deliberate practice that requires conscious intention and mindful awareness, something you have the opportunity and responsibility to choose actively every single day. It's about courageously shedding the carefully constructed masks and personas you've been wearing for years, perhaps decades, in your attempts to please others, gain approval, or meet the often overwhelming external expectations that society, family, friends, or colleagues have placed upon you.

Instead of continuing this exhausting performance, living your truth means wholeheartedly embracing and celebrating the authentic person you were always meant to be—the individual who exists beneath all the layers of conditioning, fear, and people-pleasing behaviors that may have accumulated over time.

When you genuinely begin the transformative journey of living your truth, something truly extraordinary and almost magical begins to unfold in your life. You gradually but decisively stop the exhausting charade of pretending to be someone you fundamentally are not, someone crafted to meet others' expectations rather than your own authentic nature. You stop feeling that constant nagging pressure and overwhelming need to conform to societal norms, workplace cultures, family expectations, or peer groups that never truly resonated with your core being in the first place.

As this beautiful transformation takes root and flourishes, you start to experience a profound, deep-seated sense of inner peace and unshakable confidence that radiates from within. This isn't the superficial confidence that comes from external validation or temporary achievements, but rather a solid, grounded assurance that emerges because you're no longer engaged in the draining internal battle of fighting against your own authentic nature, values, and instincts.

Instead of this constant internal conflict and self-betrayal, you discover that you're finally living in beautiful, harmonious alignment with your true self—the person you were always meant to be, free from the constraints of artificial personas and the weight of others' expectations.

But living your truth isn't always easy—in fact, it often represents one of the most challenging yet rewarding journeys you can embark upon. This path demands genuine courage that goes beyond momentary bravery; it requires the deep, sustained kind of courage that allows you to consistently show up as yourself even when the world seems to be pushing back. It calls for raw vulnerability, the willingness to let others see who you really are beneath all the carefully constructed masks and protective layers you may have built up over the years.

This transformative process means learning to speak your mind with conviction and clarity, even when your voice trembles with uncertainty or when you know your words might not be what others want to hear. It involves making deliberate choices that authentically align with your core values, your deepest beliefs, and your truest sense of self—even when those choices might seem unconventional, unpopular, or difficult to explain to those around you.

Perhaps most challenging of all, living authentically requires gradually releasing the paralyzing fear of judgment that has likely held you back for years. It means accepting the profound truth that even when you live with complete authenticity and integrity, not everyone will understand your choices, appreciate your perspective, or approve of the path you've chosen to walk—and discovering that this reality is not only acceptable but actually liberating. What matters most in this journey is not whether others approve of your authentic self, but whether you can look in the mirror with genuine pride and approve of the person staring back at you.

The Benefits of Living Authentically

When you fully embrace your authenticity and commit to living as your truest self, you open yourself up to experiencing a life of profound meaning, deeper satisfaction, and far greater fulfillment than you may have ever thought possible. The transformation that occurs when you stop performing for others and start honoring your genuine nature creates ripple effects that touch every corner of your existence. Here are some of the most powerful and life-changing benefits of courageously living your truth:

The Fear of Living Authentically

Despite all the profound benefits that come with embracing authenticity, many of us find ourselves holding back, paralyzed by a complex web of deeply rooted fears. The fear of judgment from others looms large in our minds, whispering warnings about what people might think or say if we dare to show our true selves. The fear of rejection cuts even deeper, threatening the very connections and belonging we crave as human beings. Then there's the fear of standing out from the crowd, of being different in a world that often rewards conformity and punishes those who dare to color outside the lines.

These fears feel overwhelming and all-consuming, but they are natural human responses that don't have to control the trajectory of your life or dictate the choices you make.

The anxious questions begin to multiply in your mind like shadows at dusk: What if they don't accept the real me when I finally let my guard down? What if I take this leap of faith and fail spectacularly, confirming all my worst fears about myself? What if people don't understand the choices I'm making, the path I'm choosing, or the person I'm becoming?

These are the common fears that surface when we first begin to contemplate living authentically, when we start to consider what it might mean to peel back the layers of pretense and show up as ourselves. But here's the fundamental truth that can change everything: Fear will always be there lurking in the background, but it doesn't have to stop you from moving forward.

Living authentically doesn't mean that you won't face challenges or encounter moments of deep discomfort along the way. It doesn't guarantee that you'll be shielded from rejection, harsh criticism, or the inevitable bumps and bruises that come with putting yourself out there in the world. There will still be people who don't understand your choices, who question your decisions, or who may even actively oppose the path you're walking.

But what authentic living does mean is something far more profound and transformative: You will be able to handle these challenges, setbacks, and difficult moments with a deep sense of self-assurance and inner peace that comes from being truly grounded in your truth. When you know who you are at your core and you're living in alignment with your values, beliefs, and genuine desires, external criticism loses much of its sting. The rejection that once felt devastating becomes manageable because your sense of worth isn't dependent on others' approval.

This inner foundation—this unshakable connection to your authentic self—becomes your anchor during life's inevitable storms. It's the difference between being a leaf blown about by every wind of opinion and being a tree with deep roots that can weather any season.

The more you cultivate and embrace authentic living as a daily practice, the more you'll discover that the once-paralyzing fear of judgment begins to lose its grip on your decisions and actions. What once felt like an insurmountable wall of anxiety about what others might think gradually transforms into something far more manageable—a background whisper rather than a deafening roar.

Through this process of genuine self-expression, you'll start to realize a profound truth that changes everything: The people who truly matter in your life—your real tribe, your genuine supporters, your authentic connections—will love, accept, and wholeheartedly support you for exactly who you are at your core, not for the carefully constructed, people-pleasing version of yourself that you might have felt pressured to present to the world.

These meaningful relationships, built on the foundation of your authentic self, become deeper and more fulfilling than any connection based on pretense ever could be. When you show up as your true self, you give others permission to do the same, creating a ripple effect of authenticity that strengthens every bond in your life.

Exercise: Take One Authentic Step

Living your truth is a gradual, unfolding process—it doesn't happen overnight or through a single moment of revelation. It's a journey of continuous discovery, small choices, and incremental shifts that compound over time. But within this longer journey, there are small meaningful steps you can take each day that help you live more authentically and align your actions with your deepest values and desires.

These daily acts of authenticity might seem insignificant on their own, but they create a powerful momentum that builds upon itself. Each genuine choice you make strengthens your capacity for the next one, creating a positive cycle of self-trust and authentic expression. Let's begin with one small but powerful action you can take today—a concrete step that moves you closer to living in alignment with who you truly are.

Think about an area of your life where you've been holding back from fully expressing your true self—where you've perhaps been playing it safe or conforming to what you believe others expect of you. This might be in a conversation where you've consistently chosen silence over speaking your mind, biting your tongue when you have something meaningful to contribute because you're worried about how your words might be received.

Perhaps it's within a relationship where you've been carefully concealing your true feelings, thoughts, or desires, presenting a version of yourself that feels more palatable or acceptable rather than risking the vulnerability that comes with genuine emotional honesty. Or maybe it's in your professional life, where you find yourself going through the motions in a job that doesn't align with your deeper passions and values, staying in a role that feels safe but unfulfilling because pursuing what truly matters to you seems too risky or uncertain.

Consider also those moments when you've dimmed your natural enthusiasm, modified your opinions to match the room, or suppressed aspects of your personality that make you uniquely you. These areas of self-censorship often reveal themselves in the small, everyday choices—the times when you've chosen the expected path over the authentic one, when you've prioritized keeping the peace over honoring your truth.

Now identify one small step you can take today to be more authentic in that area. Here are a few examples:

Once you've carefully considered and decided on the specific step you want to take toward greater authenticity, commit to creating a concrete, actionable plan to implement it today—not tomorrow, not next week, but right now, in this moment. It doesn't have to be a dramatic, life-altering transformation that completely overhauls your entire existence—sometimes the most profound shifts begin with just a small, seemingly insignificant act of genuine authenticity that honors who you truly are beneath all the layers of expectation and pretense.

Whether it's sending that heartfelt message you've been crafting in your mind for weeks, wearing that piece of clothing that makes you feel genuinely yourself despite what others might think, or simply speaking up in a conversation with your honest opinion instead of defaulting to what you think people want to hear, take that brave step forward. You'll be genuinely surprised and perhaps even moved by how remarkably good, how deeply satisfying and liberating it feels to finally take that concrete step toward living your authentic truth, even if it's just one small movement in the direction of the person you've always known yourself to be.

Overcoming the Fear of Rejection

One of the most formidable and paralyzing obstacles standing in the way of living authentically is the deeply rooted, almost primal fear of rejection that seems to lurk in the shadows of our consciousness. This fear manifests in countless ways throughout our daily lives—we find ourselves constantly worrying, sometimes to the point of obsession, that if we dare to show up as our genuine, unfiltered selves, exposing our true thoughts, feelings, vulnerabilities, and quirks, others will inevitably judge us harshly, criticize our choices mercilessly, or perhaps most painfully of all, simply abandon us entirely when they discover who we really are beneath the carefully constructed facade we've spent years perfecting.

The fear of rejection operates as an incredibly powerful and often overwhelming force that can dictate our every move, influencing the words we choose to speak, the clothes we decide to wear, the opinions we express or carefully suppress, and even the dreams we dare to pursue or quietly abandon. It whispers insidious doubts in our ears, convincing us that safety lies in conformity, that acceptance requires us to mold ourselves into whatever shape we believe others want us to take, regardless of how uncomfortable or unnatural that shape might feel.

However, it's absolutely crucial and liberating to understand this fundamental truth: You simply cannot control how others will respond to your authenticity, no matter how much you might wish otherwise or how carefully you try to anticipate their reactions. What you can control—and what ultimately matters most for your own well-being and sense of integrity—is how you choose to show up for yourself each and every day, whether you honor your own values and truth, and whether you have the courage to be genuinely, unapologetically yourself in a world that often seems determined to make you into someone else entirely.

People will inevitably judge you, regardless of what you do or how carefully you try to present yourself to the world—this is simply an inescapable reality of human nature and social interaction that we must all learn to accept. Some will criticize your choices, others will question your motives, and still others will form opinions based on incomplete information or their own personal biases and limitations. This judgment will happen whether you're living authentically or wearing a carefully crafted mask, whether you're following your heart or desperately trying to please everyone around you.

But here's the remarkable silver lining that makes this difficult truth worth embracing: When you make the courageous decision to live authentically, something almost magical begins to happen in your life. You start to naturally attract people who genuinely resonate with your truth, who appreciate the real you rather than some sanitized version you think they want to see. These are the individuals who will celebrate your quirks rather than judge them, who will support your dreams rather than diminish them, and who will love you for exactly who you are rather than who they think you should become.

The more courageously and consistently you embrace who you truly are—your values, your passions, your unique perspective on the world, your authentic way of being—the more powerfully you'll draw into your orbit relationships, opportunities, and experiences that are genuinely aligned with your authentic self. This magnetic effect of authenticity creates a life that feels more fulfilling, more purposeful, and infinitely more satisfying than any existence built on pretense or people-pleasing ever could.

Remember, rejection is not a reflection of your inherent worth as a human being or an indictment of your character. It's simply a clear indicator that something—whether it's a relationship, a job opportunity, a social circle, or someone's approval—wasn't the right fit for who you truly are at this moment in your journey. This misalignment doesn't diminish your value; it simply means that particular connection wasn't meant to flourish in your life.

When you courageously embrace your true self and stop contorting yourself to fit into spaces that weren't designed for your authentic essence, you free yourself from the exhausting burden of trying to please everyone around you. You release yourself from the impossible task of being all things to all people, a pursuit that inevitably leads to burnout and a profound sense of disconnection from your own truth.

In making this liberating choice, you create genuine space—both emotionally and energetically—for the right people and opportunities to naturally flow into your life. These aligned connections will recognize and celebrate your authenticity rather than requiring you to dim your light or compromise your values to earn their acceptance.

Final Thought: Your Truth Is Your Strength

Living your truth is undoubtedly one of the most profoundly empowering and transformative choices you can make in your lifetime. It represents a fundamental shift from external validation to internal alignment, from performance to presence, from hiding to wholehearted living. This choice to embrace authenticity may feel overwhelmingly difficult at first, particularly if you've spent years—perhaps even decades—carefully hiding essential parts of yourself, suppressing your genuine thoughts and feelings, or wearing masks that felt safer than vulnerability.

The journey toward authenticity often begins with small, tentative steps. You might start by expressing a previously hidden opinion in a conversation, setting a boundary you've long avoided, or simply allowing yourself to feel emotions you've been pushing down. These initial moments of truth-telling can feel terrifying, as they require you to release the familiar comfort of your protective facades and step into the unknown territory of genuine self-expression.

Yet with each courageous step you take toward authenticity, something remarkable begins to unfold within you. You'll gradually discover that you feel more vibrantly alive than you have in years, as if you're finally breathing deeply after holding your breath for far too long. You'll sense a deeper, more meaningful connection to your true purpose—that unique contribution only you can make to the world. Most importantly, you'll experience a profound sense of peace that comes from no longer fighting against your own nature, but instead flowing in harmony with who you were always meant to be.

Remember, you don't need anyone's permission to be yourself—not from family members who may have shaped your early understanding of acceptability, not from colleagues who might prefer a more palatable version of you, not from friends who've grown comfortable with the masks you've worn, and certainly not from society at large with its endless expectations and judgments. Your truth, with all its complexities and contradictions, is your greatest strength and your most powerful gift to offer the world.

When you make the brave choice to live authentically, something beautiful and transformative happens that extends far beyond your personal experience. You become a living example of what's possible when someone chooses courage over comfort, truth over convenience. Others witness your genuine self-expression—perhaps the way you speak your mind with quiet confidence, the manner in which you honor your values even when it's difficult, or simply the peaceful energy that radiates from someone who's no longer at war with themselves—and they begin to feel permission stirring within their own hearts.

You create a ripple effect that spreads outward in ways you may never fully comprehend, touching lives and awakening possibilities in people you may not even realize are watching. Each time you choose authenticity over performance, you help build a world where everyone feels increasingly free to shed their own protective layers and express their unique, irreplaceable selves with growing confidence and joy.

In the next chapter, we'll delve deep into the transformative role that self-compassion plays in helping you maintain your authentic self through life's inevitable challenges and setbacks. Living authentically isn't always easy—there will be moments when you question yourself, times when others misunderstand your choices, and periods when the weight of staying true to your values feels overwhelming.

The voice of self-doubt may whisper that it would be simpler to retreat back into familiar patterns of people-pleasing or performance. Yet with genuine compassion for yourself—the kind of gentle understanding you would offer a dear friend facing similar struggles—you can navigate those bumps in the road with grace, wisdom, and unwavering self-respect.

But for now, before we move forward together, take a moment to pause and reflect thoughtfully on your own unique journey toward authenticity. Consider how far you've already traveled from where you began, acknowledging both the small daily victories and the larger breakthroughs that have shaped who you're becoming. Notice the courage it has taken to question old patterns, to disappoint people who preferred your former self, and to keep choosing truth even when it felt uncomfortable or uncertain.

You are worthy of living your truth—not because you've earned it through achievement or approval but simply because you exist as the remarkable, complex, beautifully imperfect human being that you are. The world is waiting, perhaps more desperately than you realize, for you to show up fully as you truly are, bringing all your gifts, perspectives, and authentic presence to a reality that needs exactly what you have to offer.

Chapter 8

Surrounding Yourself with Support

The Importance of Support

Living authentically is a profound and transformative journey that touches every aspect of your existence, but it can be remarkably challenging at times, particularly when you find yourself navigating the treacherous waters of fear, persistent self-doubt, or unexpected resistance from those around you. The path to genuine self-expression is rarely smooth or straightforward, and it's during these inevitable moments of uncertainty that you might question whether you're on the right track or wonder if it would be easier to simply conform to others' expectations.

That's precisely why surrounding yourself with the right kind of support becomes not just helpful but absolutely crucial to your continued growth and well-being. The quality and nature of the relationships you cultivate can make the difference between thriving in your authenticity and feeling isolated in your struggles.

While being true to yourself is undeniably a deeply personal endeavor that requires individual courage, self-reflection, and commitment, it doesn't mean you have to shoulder this responsibility entirely alone. The misconception that authentic living is a solitary pursuit can actually hinder your progress and leave you feeling unnecessarily disconnected from others who could provide valuable perspective, encouragement, and understanding.

In fact, intentionally surrounding yourself with people who genuinely support your journey toward authenticity is absolutely essential for sustained long-term growth, emotional resilience, and lasting fulfillment. These supportive relationships become the foundation upon which you can build the confidence to continue being true to yourself, even when the path becomes difficult or uncertain.

Support doesn't emerge solely from the intimate circle of people closest to you—those family members and lifelong friends who have witnessed your journey from the beginning. Rather, meaningful support can flow from virtually anyone who genuinely uplifts your spirit, consistently encourages your growth, and demonstrates authentic respect for your unique individuality and personal choices. The beauty of building a truly robust support system lies in recognizing that it can be composed of an incredibly diverse array of relationships and connections.

This multifaceted network might include cherished friends who understand your deepest aspirations, family members who celebrate your authentic self, experienced mentors who offer wisdom and guidance based on their own journeys, supportive coworkers who appreciate your contributions and perspective in professional settings, and even vibrant online communities filled with like-minded individuals who share similar values, passions, or life goals. Each of these different types of relationships brings its own unique flavor of support, creating a rich tapestry of encouragement that can sustain you through various challenges and celebrate with you during moments of triumph.

Having a reliable, carefully cultivated support system serves as an invaluable anchor that can help you stay grounded in your authentic self, deeply motivated to pursue your genuine aspirations, and consistently reminded of your inherent worth and unique value—especially during those particularly challenging moments when the external world feels chaotic, overwhelming, or hostile to your true nature. The presence of people who truly understand and appreciate who you are at your core provides a stabilizing force that can weather even the most turbulent storms of doubt, criticism, or uncertainty.

You are fundamentally not meant to navigate the complex journey of life in complete isolation, struggling alone with your thoughts, fears, and dreams. Similarly, you absolutely don't have to carry the full weight of every challenge, setback, or difficult decision entirely on your own shoulders. The human experience is inherently communal, designed for connection and mutual support. Just as our minds and hearts require meaningful connection for optimal mental and emotional health—thriving on understanding, empathy, and genuine human bonds—we also desperately need consistent encouragement, validation, and gentle guidance to continue courageously living as our most authentic selves, particularly when societal pressures or personal doubts threaten to pull us away from our true path.

The Types of Support You Need

When it comes to identifying and cultivating the specific kind of support that truly nurtures and strengthens your authenticity, it's important to understand that genuine support extends far beyond simply having people around you who automatically agree with everything you say, think, or do. In fact, such unconditional agreement can sometimes be more harmful than helpful, creating an echo chamber that prevents real growth and self-awareness. True, meaningful support comes from those remarkable individuals who genuinely care about your overall well-being, your personal growth, and your long-term happiness—people who want to see you not just succeed in conventional terms but flourish in becoming the most authentic, fulfilled, and genuinely content version of yourself.

These supportive relationships are characterized by a deep investment in your journey toward self-discovery and personal evolution. The people who offer this invaluable support understand that sometimes caring for someone means challenging them lovingly, asking difficult questions, or providing perspectives that might initially feel uncomfortable but ultimately serve your highest good. They recognize that authentic support requires both compassion and courage—the compassion to hold space for your struggles and the courage to speak truth when necessary.

This profound kind of support manifests itself in various meaningful forms, each serving a unique and essential role in your personal development and authentic self-expression.

Cultivating Supportive Relationships

Creating a robust and meaningful network of genuinely supportive people begins with the conscious, intentional effort to actively seek out and cultivate relationships that truly nourish, validate, and celebrate your most authentic self. This process requires both discernment and patience as you learn to distinguish between surface-level connections and those deeper bonds that offer real sustenance for your soul.

Whether these invaluable individuals manifest in your life as loving family members who accept you unconditionally, trusted friends who stand by you through life's inevitable ups and downs, wise mentors who guide your personal and professional development, or understanding colleagues who appreciate your unique contributions and perspective, the people who genuinely support you should consistently encourage you to embrace and express your true self—without harsh judgment, unrealistic expectations, or pressure to conform to their own vision of who you should be.

These relationships become the foundation upon which authentic living can flourish, providing the emotional security and encouragement necessary for you to take risks, explore new possibilities, and grow into the person you're meant to become. Here are some thoughtful and practical steps to begin cultivating these transformative relationships:

Navigating Negative or Unsupportive Relationships

Not all relationships will support your authenticity journey, and that's a difficult but essential truth you need to accept as you continue growing into your most genuine self. Some people in your life may carry their own deep-seated insecurities, unresolved fears, or limiting beliefs that cause them to react negatively, defensively, or even hostilely to your personal growth or your conscious decision to live more authentically. These reactions often stem from their own discomfort with change, their fear of being left behind, or their unconscious recognition that your transformation might highlight areas where they themselves feel stuck or unfulfilled.

Others may simply not understand or appreciate the significant changes you're making in your life, particularly if they've grown accustomed to seeing you behave, think, or respond in predictable patterns that served their expectations or needs. When you begin shifting away from people-pleasing behaviors, standing up for your values, or making choices that prioritize your well-being over others' comfort, some individuals may feel confused, threatened, or even betrayed by this evolution.

These relationship challenges can feel particularly painful when they involve family members, long-term friends, or colleagues who you hoped would celebrate your growth. The disappointment of discovering that someone you care about cannot or will not support your authentic journey can create feelings of loneliness, doubt, or even guilt about your choices.

Dealing with these complex and often emotionally charged unsupportive relationships requires a delicate balance of compassionate understanding and firm assertiveness. You must learn to protect your authentic self while still maintaining your integrity and emotional well-being. Here's how to navigate these challenging situations with grace and strength:

Exercise: Building Your Support Network

It's time to take a deliberate and honest look at your current support system, examining the various relationships that shape your daily experience and influence your journey toward authentic living. Start by creating a quiet space for yourself where you can engage in thoughtful reflection about the people in your life and how they genuinely affect your personal growth, emotional well-being, and your ability to express your true self without fear or hesitation.

Consider setting aside dedicated time to deeply contemplate these relationships, perhaps with a journal or notebook nearby to capture your insights. As you embark on this important self-assessment, write down the following observations and reflections:

Final Thought: You Are Not Alone

You are not meant to navigate the complex and often challenging journey toward authenticity in complete isolation, carrying the weight of self-discovery and personal transformation entirely on your own shoulders. The path to becoming your truest self requires courage, vulnerability, and persistent effort, but it doesn't have to be a solitary struggle filled with doubt and uncertainty. Instead, actively seek out and intentionally surround yourself with people who genuinely encourage your growth, celebrate your uniqueness, and inspire you to become the most authentic and empowered version of yourself—individuals who see your potential even when you struggle to recognize it within yourself.

These meaningful relationships that consistently nurture your personal growth, provide unwavering emotional comfort during difficult moments, and offer the kind of unconditional love that doesn't depend on your performance or achievements are absolutely vital for your overall well-being and lasting happiness. Such connections serve as anchors of stability when the winds of change threaten to overwhelm you, and they become sources of strength that remind you of your inherent worth when self-doubt attempts to derail your progress toward living authentically.

Remember, authenticity is not merely about living for yourself in isolation or pursuing self-interest without regard for others—it's fundamentally about creating and cultivating a rich, meaningful life that genuinely reflects who you are at your core, and that profound journey often involves courageously sharing your deepest truths, values, and experiences with the people around you. When you deliberately and thoughtfully surround yourself with individuals who not only accept but actively support, encourage, and celebrate your authentic self-expression, you naturally become significantly more empowered, confident, and inspired to live your truth boldly, openly, and without apology or compromise.

This supportive network becomes a foundation that allows you to express yourself with greater freedom and less fear of judgment, knowing that your authentic voice and genuine presence are valued and welcomed by those who matter most in your life.

In the upcoming chapter, we'll delve deeply into the transformative ways that self-compassion serves as a cornerstone for maintaining your authentic self, particularly during those inevitable moments when life presents you with significant obstacles, setbacks, or periods of uncertainty that might otherwise shake your confidence in who you truly are. We'll examine how treating yourself with the same kindness and understanding you would offer a cherished friend becomes essential for navigating the complex journey of authentic living.

But for this present moment, as you reflect on everything we've discussed about building meaningful connections, please hold close to your heart the fundamental truth that you absolutely deserve genuine support, deep understanding, and authentic connection in your life. The right people—those who truly see and appreciate your authentic self—will not only encourage you to remain true to your core values and beliefs but will actively help you stay anchored to your genuine identity, even when external pressures or internal doubts attempt to pull you away from your authentic path.

Chapter 9

You Are Enough—Embracing Your True Self

The Journey to Self-Acceptance

Throughout this book, we've journeyed together through the intricate landscape of what it truly means to live authentically—to strip away the masks we wear, the expectations we carry, and the false narratives we tell ourselves about who we should be. We've explored how embracing your genuine self, in all its complexity and imperfection, can bring about a life overflowing with fulfillment, deep-rooted purpose, and lasting inner peace.

We've delved into the transformative importance of self-compassion, learning to treat ourselves with the same kindness we would offer a dear friend facing struggles. We've examined the toxic nature of comparison and how releasing ourselves from the exhausting game of measuring our worth against others can free us to celebrate our unique path. We've discovered the profound joy that comes from identifying and pursuing your true passions—those activities and interests that make your soul come alive and remind you of who you are beneath all the noise.

We've also discussed the vital importance of surrounding yourself with positive energy, creating boundaries that protect your peace, and cultivating relationships that nourish rather than drain your spirit. Each of these elements has been a crucial piece of the puzzle, a stepping stone on the path toward authentic living.

But all these steps, all these insights and practices, ultimately culminate in one beautifully simple yet profound truth that forms the foundation of everything else: You are enough.

This is the profound essence of everything we've explored together throughout these pages. No matter where you currently find yourself on your personal journey of self-discovery, no matter the mistakes you've made along the way or the seemingly insurmountable challenges you're facing in this very moment, you are enough exactly as you are, right now, in this present breath. You are complete, whole, and worthy of love and acceptance—not because of what you've achieved or accomplished but simply because you exist as the unique, irreplaceable human being that you are.

Living authentically doesn't mean you have to have it all figured out or maintain some impossible standard of perfection. It's not about having a flawless track record, making all the right decisions, or presenting a polished version of yourself to the world at every moment. Rather, it means wholeheartedly embracing the raw, unvarnished beauty of who you truly are—accepting every quirk, every vulnerability, every perceived flaw, and every beautiful imperfection that makes you uniquely you.

It means courageously showing up in the world as your complete, unfiltered, genuine self, without masks or pretenses, knowing deep in your heart that you possess inherent worth and immeasurable value—not because of what you do, what you own, or how others perceive you but simply because you exist as a conscious, breathing, feeling human being with your own irreplaceable story to tell.

This final chapter serves as a gentle, powerful reminder that you don't need to fundamentally transform yourself, reinvent your personality, or become someone entirely different to earn love, acceptance, or validation from others. You don't need to contort yourself into impossible shapes or sacrifice your authentic nature to fit into boxes that others have constructed for you. The truth that resonates at the very core of your being is that you already possess everything you need—every quality, every strength, every piece of wisdom, every ounce of resilience—to live a life that is genuinely full of purpose, deep inner peace, and abundant joy.

You don't need to wait for some future version of yourself to emerge before you can claim your worthiness. You don't need to achieve certain milestones, accumulate specific accomplishments, or reach particular benchmarks before you're allowed to feel complete and whole. The foundation for a meaningful, fulfilling existence already exists within you, waiting to be recognized, honored, and expressed in all its authentic glory.

The Power of Self-Acceptance

Self-acceptance stands as the fundamental cornerstone of authentic living, the bedrock upon which all genuine self-expression and meaningful relationships are built. It represents the profound, life-altering understanding that permeates every aspect of your existence—the deep recognition that regardless of your complicated past, the weight of your accumulated mistakes, the lingering shadows of your insecurities, or the messy imperfections that seem to follow you through life, you remain inherently and unquestionably worthy of love, respect, dignity, and happiness.

This transformative concept of self-acceptance isn't about surrendering your aspirations, abandoning your dreams, or giving up entirely on personal growth and improvement. It's not a passive resignation to mediocrity or an excuse to remain stagnant in patterns that no longer serve you. Rather, it's about cultivating the courage and wisdom to accept yourself completely and unconditionally—exactly where you are right now, in this very moment, with all your complexities and contradictions—while still maintaining an open heart and holding generous space for meaningful change, continuous learning, and purposeful progress.

True self-acceptance means embracing the beautiful paradox of being simultaneously complete and evolving, whole and growing, enough and becoming.

When you truly accept yourself with all your complexities and contradictions, you naturally release the exhausting, soul-draining need for constant validation from others. You gradually stop looking desperately for approval from friends, family, colleagues, or strangers, and you cease the relentless, anxiety-inducing effort of constantly trying to meet the ever-shifting external expectations that society, your culture, or other people place upon you.

Instead, you begin to trust yourself deeply and implicitly—trusting your instincts, your judgment, your inner wisdom, and your capacity to navigate life's complexities. You start making deliberate, conscious choices that genuinely align with your core values, your authentic passions, and your unique sense of purpose, rather than decisions driven by fear, people-pleasing, or the desperate desire to fit into someone else's vision of who you should be.

Self-acceptance is profoundly liberating in ways that touch every aspect of your existence. It bestows upon you the precious, hard-won freedom to be beautifully, authentically imperfect—to stumble, to make mistakes, to experience setbacks, and to occasionally fall short of your own expectations without being consumed by the crushing weight of self-criticism or paralyzed by the fear of harsh judgment from others.

This freedom extends far beyond mere tolerance of your flaws; it encompasses a genuine appreciation for your humanity. It grants you permission to fail spectacularly sometimes, to take risks that don't always pay off, to pursue dreams that might not materialize exactly as you envisioned, and to continue growing, learning, and evolving at your own unique pace without the constant, exhausting pressure of needing to prove your worthiness to anyone—including yourself.

When you truly embrace self-acceptance, you begin to see yourself as inherently whole and complete, worthy of love and respect exactly as you are in this moment, even while you remain actively engaged in the beautiful, ongoing process of becoming who you're meant to be. You recognize that your value isn't contingent on reaching some distant finish line of perfection but rather exists as an unchanging truth woven into the very fabric of your being.

Embracing Your Imperfections

One of the most formidable and pervasive barriers standing firmly in the way of genuine self-acceptance is the deeply ingrained, culturally reinforced idea that we must somehow achieve an impossible state of flawless perfection in every aspect of our lives. This insidious belief system permeates nearly every corner of our modern society, which consistently bombards us with carefully curated images of success, relentlessly tells us through countless channels and voices that to be truly successful, genuinely loved, or authentically valued by others, we must somehow manage to have absolutely everything figured out—our careers perfectly mapped, our relationships harmoniously balanced, our personal lives immaculately organized, and our emotional responses consistently measured and appropriate.

The media presents us with airbrushed versions of reality, social platforms showcase only the highlight reels of others' lives, and we find ourselves constantly measuring our behind-the-scenes struggles against everyone else's carefully polished public performances. We're led to believe that somewhere out there, people exist who have achieved this mythical state of having it all together, never doubting themselves, never making poor decisions, never experiencing moments of confusion or uncertainty.

But the profound, liberating truth that can transform your entire relationship with yourself is this: Perfection doesn't exist anywhere in the human experience. It never has, and it never will. We are all—every single one of us, without exception—magnificent works in progress, constantly evolving, perpetually learning, forever growing and changing. Our perceived imperfections, those very qualities we spend so much energy trying to hide or fix, are precisely what make us beautifully, authentically human. They are the threads that weave the rich tapestry of our individual stories, the brushstrokes that create the unique masterpiece of who we are.

Embracing your imperfections means wholeheartedly accepting that you will inevitably make mistakes along the way, experience unexpected setbacks that knock you off course, and face challenges that test your resolve and push you beyond your comfort zone. But it also means recognizing with deep understanding that these very experiences—the stumbles, the detours, the moments of uncertainty—are not obstacles to your growth but rather integral, essential parts of it.

Each mistake you make becomes a precious opportunity to learn something new about yourself, about others, or about the world around you. These errors in judgment or missteps in execution are not failures of character but rather invaluable lessons wrapped in momentary disappointment. Each challenge that presents itself in your path is truly a chance to discover inner strength you didn't know you possessed, to develop resilience you never thought possible, and to become a more capable, more confident version of yourself.

Each failure, no matter how painful or embarrassing it might feel in the moment, serves as a crucial stepping stone toward the success you're building. These setbacks create the foundation upon which your future achievements will stand, providing you with the wisdom, experience, and determination that can only come from having weathered life's storms and emerged stronger on the other side.

When you truly accept your imperfections with genuine compassion and understanding, you finally stop holding yourself to those impossibly high, unrealistic standards that have been weighing you down for so long. You grant yourself the precious permission to be vulnerable, to expose your authentic self to the world without the heavy armor of pretense, to courageously try new things even when success isn't guaranteed, and to stumble and fail without the crushing burden of shame or self-condemnation.

You begin to understand with crystal clarity that your mistakes—those moments of poor judgment, those times when things don't go according to plan, those instances when you fall short of your own expectations—don't define your fundamental worth as a human being. They don't diminish your value or make you any less deserving of love, respect, and happiness. Instead, you recognize that these missteps are simply natural, inevitable parts of the human journey, threads woven into the rich tapestry of a life lived fully and authentically.

Exercise: Affirm Your Worth

Now that you've explored the profound importance of genuine self-acceptance and begun to understand its transformative power in your life, let's take a meaningful moment to pause and deliberately affirm your inherent worth as a human being. Self-affirmations, when crafted thoughtfully and spoken with genuine intention, are an incredibly powerful and accessible tool in reinforcing your deep sense of self-worth, building unshakable confidence from within, and creating a foundation of self-compassion that will support you through life's inevitable ups and downs.

Take some quiet time to write down a comprehensive list of personal affirmations that truly remind you of your unique value, celebrate your individual strengths and talents, acknowledge your remarkable resilience, and honor the beautiful uniqueness that makes you who you are. These aren't empty platitudes or wishful thinking—they are truthful statements about your worth that deserve to be acknowledged, spoken aloud, and deeply internalized.

Here are some examples to get you started:

Repeat these powerful affirmations daily, especially during those moments when self-doubt creeps in and you're feeling unsure of yourself, your capabilities, or your worth. Speak them aloud with deep conviction and unwavering confidence, letting each word resonate through your entire being, knowing with absolute certainty that you are speaking nothing but the profound truth about who you are.

Allow these words to settle into your heart and mind, becoming part of your internal dialogue and daily practice. You are inherently worthy of love, respect, and happiness. You are completely enough, exactly as you are in this moment. You are deserving of all the abundant love, joy, success, and beautiful opportunities that life has to offer and that are already making their way into your experience.

Living Authentically Every Day

Living authentically isn't just about grand gestures or monumental life transformations—it's about the small, seemingly insignificant daily decisions that consistently align with who you truly are at your core. It's about making conscious choices, both big and small, that genuinely reflect your deepest values, your burning passions, your authentic desires, and the essence of who you are when no one else is watching.

This authentic living manifests in countless everyday moments: choosing to speak up when something doesn't feel right, even when it would be easier to stay silent; selecting clothes that make you feel comfortable and confident rather than what's trending; pursuing hobbies and interests that genuinely spark joy within you, regardless of whether others understand or appreciate them; setting boundaries that protect your energy and well-being, even when it disappoints others; and making career decisions based on what fulfills you rather than what looks impressive on paper or meets external expectations.

Each small act of authenticity builds upon the last, creating a foundation of self-trust and integrity that strengthens over time. When you consistently honor your true self in these daily choices, you begin to live a life that feels genuinely yours—one that reflects your unique perspective, values, and dreams rather than a pale imitation of what you think you should be.

Living authentically requires dedicated, intentional practice—it's not something that happens overnight or comes naturally to most people. It requires you to deliberately step outside your carefully constructed comfort zone, to willingly embrace the raw vulnerability that comes with showing your true self to the world, and to summon the deep, unwavering courage to be genuinely yourself, even when it feels terrifying and uncertain.

It means consciously letting go of the paralyzing fear of judgment from others—that constant voice in your head questioning whether you're doing enough, being enough, or measuring up to invisible standards. This journey demands that you develop an unshakable trust in the fact that your authentic self, with all its imperfections and complexities, is not only enough but exactly what the world needs from you.

Here are some ways you can practice living authentically every day:

Final Thought: You Are the Author of Your Story

You hold the pen to your own life with unwavering certainty, grasping it firmly in your hands as you craft each chapter with deliberate intention. You are the author of your story, the sole architect of your narrative, and you possess the inherent power to shape every twist, turn, and triumph that unfolds across the pages of your existence. This isn't merely a metaphor—it's a fundamental truth that deserves to be embraced with both courage and conviction.

You don't need to conform to anyone else's rigid expectations or carefully follow someone else's well-worn path, no matter how successful or appealing it might appear from the outside. Those paths were carved by different feet, shaped by different dreams, and guided by different visions of what constitutes a meaningful life. Your journey is uniquely yours, with its own rhythm, its own lessons, and its own magnificent destination.

You are the only one who truly knows what's best for you, who understands the quiet whispers of your heart and the persistent calling of your soul. You possess an inner wisdom that has been cultivated through your experiences, your struggles, your victories, and your moments of profound clarity. Your truth—authentic, unfiltered, and deeply personal—is the only one that truly matters in determining the direction of your life and the legacy you choose to create.

Remember, authenticity is a profound and ongoing journey rather than a fixed destination you can simply arrive at and claim as conquered. This path toward genuine self-expression will inevitably present you with moments of deep uncertainty and piercing doubt, where the voice of criticism—both internal and external—may attempt to pull you away from your chosen course. You will encounter significant challenges that test your resolve, unexpected setbacks that temporarily shake your confidence, and periods where the easier path of conformity seems far more appealing than the sometimes lonely road of authentic living.

Yet with each deliberate step you courageously take toward honoring and living your fundamental truth, you'll discover something remarkable beginning to unfold within the fabric of your daily existence. You'll find a deeper, more sustainable sense of peace settling into the corners of your mind that were once occupied by anxiety and self-doubt. A more genuine and lasting joy will begin to permeate your experiences, replacing the hollow satisfaction that comes from meeting others' expectations. Most importantly, you'll encounter a profound sense of fulfillment that can only emerge when your outer actions align perfectly with your inner values and deepest convictions.

You don't have to achieve some impossible standard of perfection, nor do you need to have every aspect of your life flawlessly organized before you can be truly worthy of love, respect, and remarkable success. You are inherently enough, possessing infinite value and potential exactly as you are in this very moment, with all your beautiful imperfections, ongoing struggles, and works-in-progress that make you uniquely human.

As you continue to walk this transformative path with increasing confidence and self-awareness, remember that you are never truly alone in this journey of self-discovery and authentic living. You are an integral part of a vast, interconnected world filled with countless individuals who are also courageously seeking their own authenticity, desperately yearning for genuine acceptance, and searching for the kind of unconditional love that validates their true essence. Each person you encounter, whether briefly in passing or deeply through meaningful relationships, carries within them their own struggles with self-acceptance, their own dreams of living authentically, and their own profound desire to be seen and valued for who they really are beneath the masks and pretenses.

By consistently choosing to embrace and honor your true self, especially in moments when it feels vulnerable or challenging to do so, you become a living beacon of possibility for others who are still trapped in the exhausting cycle of trying to be someone they're not. Your courage to show up authentically in the world sends powerful ripples of inspiration outward, touching lives in ways you may never fully realize or comprehend. When others witness your commitment to living your truth, they begin to believe that such freedom might also be possible for them, creating an ever-expanding ripple effect of positivity, genuine self-love, and authentic connection that has the profound potential to gradually transform communities, relationships, and ultimately change the very fabric of our world.

You are enough, completely and utterly enough, exactly as you are in this moment. You always have been enough, even in your darkest hours of self-doubt, and you always will be enough, regardless of what challenges or triumphs lie ahead on your unique path.

This is the final chapter of this particular story, but understand that your personal journey toward complete self-acceptance and authentic living is truly just beginning to unfold in all its magnificent complexity. Keep moving forward with unwavering determination and gentle self-compassion, consistently embracing your unique authenticity even when the path feels uncertain or challenging, and always knowing deep in your heart that every single step you courageously take toward living your deepest truth—no matter how small or seemingly insignificant—is actually a profound victory worth celebrating.

You are inherently worthy of all the incredible greatness, boundless joy, meaningful connections, and extraordinary experiences that life has to offer, not because of what you achieve or accomplish but simply because you exist as the remarkable, irreplaceable human being you were always meant to be.

About the Author

Travis James Brown is a forty-three-year-old Army veteran, married, and the proud father of four. Living in the serene landscapes of rural Missouri, Travis is dedicated to his work as a psychiatric mental health nurse practitioner, where he helps others navigate the complexities of mental health. In his personal life, he finds joy in spending quality time with his family, enjoying sports, and indulging in fishing. A passionate writer, Travis has a vivid imagination and a deep love for storytelling. Through his writing, he shares his unique perspectives and creates gripping narratives, often exploring themes of action, suspense, and deep emotional connections. His stories reflect not only his creativity but also his desire to connect with others through the power of storytelling. Outside of work and family, Travis enjoys the peaceful outdoors, often casting his line in the calm waters while reflecting on his experiences and the world around him. His life is a balance of caring for others, engaging in his passions, and nurturing a close-knit family that shares in his love of adventure and creativity.

www.ingramcontent.com/pod-product-compliance
Lightning Source LLC
LaVergne TN
LVHW090425210926
848480LV00002B/688